LOCH LOM
TRO!

THE GUIDE BUUR

First published in 2012
by
Aird Trading (publishing)
www.scotlandbooks.co.uk
www.scotlandguidebooks.co.uk

Authors: Lynne Woods & Doug Vickers
Field Assistants: Lance Jackson & Chris Woods

Copyright © Aird Trading 2012

ISBN 978-0-9562126-3-4

Cover picture: "Maid of The Loch" at Balloch Pier

INTRODUCTION

Welcome to "Loch Lomond & The Trossachs: The Guide Book", another in the series "See it...Do it....Don't miss it". The aim of each of these books is to help visitors to do just that; to make the most of their stay in a given area. This corner of Scotland is arguably one of its most visited: Being more readily accessible from the south, it is within an easy drive of the heavily populated central belt of Scotland as well as Northern England. Consequently, the area sees many day-trippers as well as those arriving for a longer stay. It can be busy along the key routes in summer but this should not deter prospective visitors – it is not necessary to venture far from the main road to discover less crowded but equally stunning scenery. There is room for everyone and we hope that in this, as with the other books in this series, we may point out all the major attractions but also encourage you to explore "off the beaten track" to discover places you might not otherwise have found.

The book is divided into sections, arranged in a logical order for touring either part or all of the area. This part of the country does not naturally separate neatly into sections: The simplest way to cover the area is to describe the long stretch along the western shore of Loch Lomond and then a series of loops or shorter stretches of road for the remaining parts. The numbers on the map on page 4 correspond with the numbered sections of the book. Please note that our maps are not intended for precision navigation – their purpose is to illustrate the general location of things mentioned in the text. An index of place names for easy reference is included on page 72. Inside the back cover you will find a list of appropriate Ordnance Survey maps. Where used, six figure numbers prefixed by "GR" refer to grid references on such maps. There is also a list of useful telephone numbers. Public toilets are listed in red in most sections. We have tried to do this as accurately as possible but in recent years many public toilets in Scotland have been closed. In some cases village community halls have stepped into the breach and made their facilities available to travellers. In other places "comfort partnerships" have been agreed with hotels who make their toilets available to non patrons – look out for signs. We have included some places where internet access is available but this is changing so rapidly that it is not possible to be totally comprehensive.

Whilst every attempt has been made to ensure accuracy, things do change with the creation of new enterprises and the disappearance of others as people retire or move on, a fact for which the publishers cannot accept responsibility.

If this is the first time you have followed one of our guide books, we hope that it will enable you to make the most of your time around Loch Lomond and The Trossachs and that it creates a wish to return soon.

CONTENTS

Page   (Red numbers refer to the area map on page 4.)

Loch Lomond & The Trossachs ..... room for everyone.

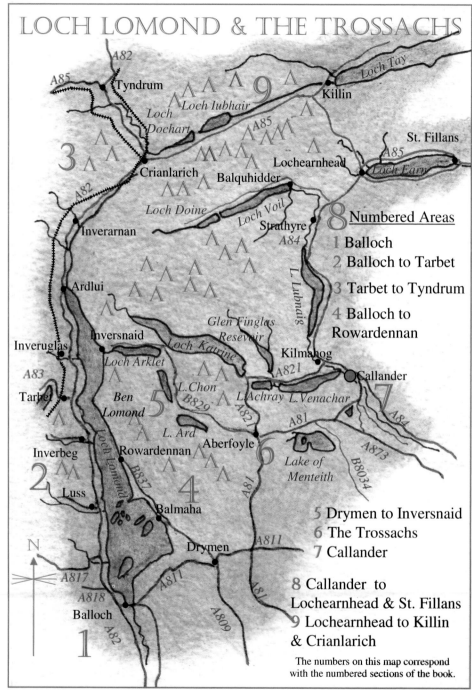

LOCH LOMOND & THE TROSSACHS

Numbered Areas

1 Balloch
2 Balloch to Tarbet
3 Tarbet to Tyndrum
4 Balloch to Rowardennan
5 Drymen to Inversnaid
6 The Trossachs
7 Callander
8 Callander to Lochearnhead & St. Fillans
9 Lochearnhead to Killin & Crianlarich

The numbers on this map correspond
with the numbered sections of the book.

WELCOME TO THE AREA

Loch Lomond takes its name from mighty Ben Lomond beneath which it stretches. It is Britain's largest expanse of fresh water and its third deepest after Lochs Morar and Ness. It is over twenty miles (32km) long and ranges in width from less than a mile (1.6km) to over four miles (7km) at the southern end, which is dotted with many islands. Most of these are privately owned although some are accessible.

Steeped in myth and legend, the area has at various times been a land of saints, poets, rogues and artists - Robert The Bruce, William Wallace, Rob Roy MacGregor and Sir Walter Scott have roamed this land and shaped its rich history, along with the many clans who have fought for local dominance. Queen Victoria also made several visits.

Most of the area covered by this book falls within the Loch Lomond & The Trossachs National Park, much of which is the Queen Elizabeth Forest Park, created in 1953 to mark the Queen's Coronation. In addition, the Ben Lomond National Memorial Park encompasses Ben Lomond down to the loch shore and is dedicated to those who lost their lives during the two World Wars. The entire National Park is a vast, natural outdoor facility with picnic areas, visitor centres, forest drives and trails for walking and cycling. The National Parks Authority and The Forestry Commission work together to ensure that the area is managed and protected for the enjoyment of all, with an emphasis on understanding the environment, encouraging its sympathetic use and protecting it for future generations.

Loch Lomond's western shores are followed by the main A82 road which runs its full length from Balloch in the south to Ardlui in the north. The eastern shore does not have a single continuous road and much of it is inaccessible except on foot or by boat. The shores on both sides of the loch provide a vast playground for boating enthusiasts but further afield are areas of great beauty and tranquillity. The Highland Boundary Fault crosses the area, dividing highlands from lowlands. The Trossachs, described as "The Highlands in miniature", are delightful with craggy peaks and shimmering lochs. The northern part of the area is Breadalbane, its wild and rugged terrain a favourite with climbers.

Loch Lomond & Ben Lomond

"Balloch" (Gaelic "Bealach") describes a place of passing: The River Leven provides a route between Loch Lomond and the Firth of Clyde. From the Middle Ages, Balloch was a gathering place on the cattle droving route south. When the railway arrived in 1850 it became a tourist destination. Situated at the southern tip of Loch Lomond, Balloch is still a gateway; to one of Scotland's iconic stretches of water, to one of its National Parks and to The Highlands themselves.

Loch Lomond Shores, open daily from 10.00am, is a prestigious retail complex with a shopping mall, several cafés, restaurants and a cocktail bar.

Loch Lomond Shores

The Gateway Centre provides visitor information and also contains Café On The Loch, an ice cream parlour, gift shop and a

The Gateway Centre

soft play area. The centre offers internet access and a ticketing service for facilities within The National Park.

Loch Lomond Sea Life Aquarium is housed in the eye-catching Drumkinnon Tower, designed by modern Scottish architect David Page to reflect Scotland's ancient strongholds.

Children's attractions include a wooden playground, crazy golf and a miniature train.

Loch Lomond Boat Hire operates from the Lagoon. Apr. – end of Oct. Tel: 07827 931 448

"Can You Experience Loch Lomond?" These people take fun seriously! Canoeing, power kiting, and abseiling, hire of bikes, canoes or pedal boats. Their "4Bs" (boats, boots, bike and bus) service will transport boots or wheels to different parts of the loch. Tel: 01389 756251

Balloch Pier
A short distance beyond Loch Lomond Shores, this was once the site of a busy railway station where passengers alighted for a trip on one of the steamers which operated on the loch.

Maid of The Loch, moored at the pier, was the last paddle steamer built in Britain and the largest ever to sail on inland waters. She was built in Glasgow by A & J. Inglis, dismantled, transported by train to Balloch then reassembled and launched on March 5th 1953.

Maid of The Loch

She remained in service until 1981 then left to deteriorate until 1966 when a group of enthusiasts determined to restore her. When fully restored she will resume service. Admission free, donations welcome. For opening hours check www.maidoftheloch.com

Steam Winch House
The nearby restored winch house of the Balloch Steam Company, erected in 1902 and restored in 2006, contains the original steam engine and winding gear.

Balloch Steam Winch House

The Duncan Mills Memorial Slipway is dedicated to the memory of Duncan Mills, the first chairman of the Loch Lomond Regional Park Authority. It is the main public slipway and the base for the National Park Rangers who work around the loch and on patrol boats.

The National Park Ranger Service. Tel: 01389 722633

Loch Lomond Water Ski Club operates from the pier during the summer months. Tel: 01436 860632.

VisitScotland Information Centre in the old station building Tel: 01389 753533

Loch Cruises
There is a wide choice of cruises available from different places on the loch, as well as a hop on – hop off water bus service.

Loch Lomond Water Bus provides a wonderful way to explore Loch Lomond, linking Balloch to other places (mid May to end of Aug.) Timetable & tickets from The Gateway Centre.

Sweeney's Cruises have been carrying visitors up and down the loch for over one hundred and twenty years. All boats have toilet and bar facilities. Booking office - by the bridge in the centre of Balloch.

Balloch Village has a a wide choice of places to eat.

Balloch House has offered loch-side accommodation since the 19th century. This was once the departure point for the River Leven Ferry. An extensive and reasonably priced menu is served by welcoming and efficient staff. (The home made fish cakes are particularly good.)

Corries Licensed Restaurant offers excellent value for money.

Palombo's Fish Restaurant serves award winning Scottish fish and chips. (Gluten free version available.) Breakfast is served from 9.00am (10.00am in winter) and there is a full menu available all day. B and B available.

The Tullie Inn is a popular restaurant and bar with accommodation.

The Waterhouse Inn is a family-run, traditional pub with a modern café bar. Food is home-made, including a tasty steak pie. Fresh fish daily.

The Dog House is a friendly pub with two bars, Skye Sports and free Wi-Fi.

The Lomond Park Hotel: The Raffles Restaurant has a reputation for reasonably priced meals and breakfast served until midday for late risers! Nightclub at weekends.

Keystore, in the centre of the village, stays open until late and sells just about everything.

Balloch Castle Country Park: The original 13th century castle was the stronghold of the Lennox family. In 1425 almost all Lennox males were executed by James 1 as reprisal for their part in his imprisonment in England prior to being

Balloch Castle

crowned. The present castle was built in 1808 for John Ardoch of Buchanan. Two hundred acres of landscaped grounds slope down to the shore. The Gothic style turreted castle has a small bell tower, complete with bell and an attractive clock. Now owned by Glasgow City Council, the castle is not open to the public but the grounds are enjoyed by locals and visitors alike - wide open spaces dotted with mature trees including a number of large, old holly trees with beautifully gnarled trunks.

Parking – free car park on Drymen Road or in the grounds (signposted from the end of Drymen Road.)

The West Loch Lomond Cycle Path runs 17 miles (27km) between Balloch and Tarbet. Much of it follows the old, disused road among the rowan, birch and alder which line the loch shore. The cycleway is also ideal for walkers, wheelchairs and pushchairs. The National Park produces an excellent leaflet/route map.

Antartex Village: Just south of Balloch, this is retail therapy on a grand scale! Outlets include "The Spirit of Scotland" whisky shop, a tartan shop, a large kitchenware department, an Edinburgh Woollen Mill store and The Village Restaurant serving good value food all day.

Loch Lomond Shooting School at Tullichewan Farm offers clay pigeon shooting and can arrange falconry, canoeing, cycle hire or guided cycling, archery and quad biking. Booking : Tel: 01389 711190

Public Toilets
The Mall, Lomond Shores.
Balloch: near the Co-op.
Balloch Castle Country Park
Internet/Wi-Fi Access
The Gateway Centre, Lomond Shores
The Dog House, Balloch

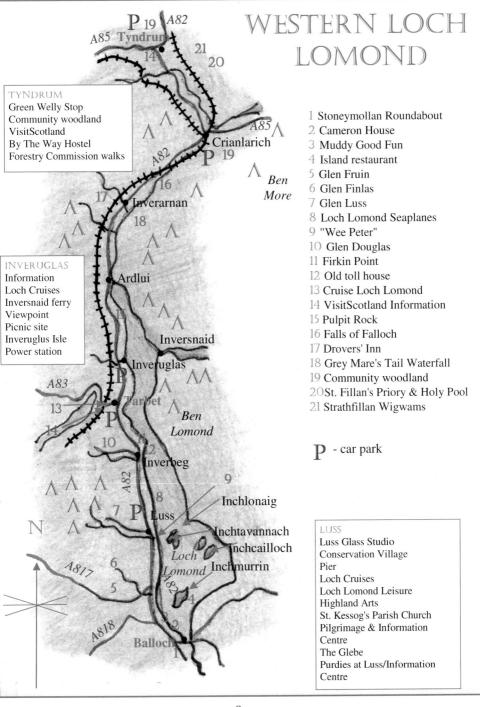

WESTERN LOCH LOMOND

9

TYNDRUM
Green Welly Stop
Community woodland
VisitScotland
By The Way Hostel
Forestry Commission walks

INVERUGLAS
Information
Loch Cruises
Inversnaid ferry
Viewpoint
Picnic site
Inveruglus Isle
Power station

1 Stoneymollan Roundabout
2 Cameron House
3 Muddy Good Fun
4 Island restaurant
5 Glen Fruin
6 Glen Finlas
7 Glen Luss
8 Loch Lomond Seaplanes
9 "Wee Peter"
10 Glen Douglas
11 Firkin Point
12 Old toll house
13 Cruise Loch Lomond
14 VisitScotland Information
15 Pulpit Rock
16 Falls of Falloch
17 Drovers' Inn
18 Grey Mare's Tail Waterfall
19 Community woodland
20 St. Fillan's Priory & Holy Pool
21 Strathfillan Wigwams

P - car park

LUSS
Luss Glass Studio
Conservation Village
Pier
Loch Cruises
Loch Lomond Leisure
Highland Arts
St. Kessog's Parish Church
Pilgrimage & Information
Centre
The Glebe
Purdies at Luss/Information
Centre

Tyndrum
Crianlarich
Inverarnan
Ben More
Ardlui
Inversnaid
Inveruglas
Tarbet
Ben Lomond
Inverbeg
Inchlonaig
Luss
Inchtavannach
Inchcailloch
Loch Lomond
Inchmurrin
Balloch

N

The **Stoneymollan Roundabout** on the A82 features flying geese against beams of glulam –layers of wood glued with the grains all running in the same direction.

Cameron House: The name derives from the Celtic "Cam Sron," a crooked nose – the shape of the headland. This was Colquhoun land until 1763, then owned by the Telfer Smollett family, Dumbarton merchants and shipbuilders.

Cameron House

Amidst lawns sloping down to the loch, Cameron House is the centre piece of a luxurious De Vere resort with time-share lodges, a marina and two golf courses.

Cameron House is a comfortable and welcoming place to stay or eat. The Boat House in the grounds offers dining in a marina setting.

The Boat House

Muddy Good Fun, based at Cameron House, offers outdoor adventures for all; shooting, archery, quad bikes, canoeing, segway safari etc. www.muddygoodfun.com

Along the A82 are several large lay-bys and picnic areas overlooking the loch.

Duck Bay Hotel & Restaurant enjoys wonderful views, contemporary decor, friendly staff and an imaginative but not fussy menu. (Smoked haddock in a creamy cheese and chive sauce is lovely!)

Outside Dining at Duck Bay

The Curiosity Shop sells quality giftware and a quirky collection of ducks. (Well, this is Duck Bay!) Open daily all year from 10.00 am.

From Arden roundabout, the A818 branches off to Helensburgh and the Clyde Sea Lochs Trail.

Inchmurrin ("Island of hospitality") is Britain's largest inland island, once a shooting estate of the Duke of Montrose. Visitors are welcome to its unique restaurant or self catering lodges. A ferry runs from a small jetty signposted from the Arden roundabout. The island is a magical place with ancient woodlands, the remains of a 7th century monastery and a 14th century castle, once a stronghold of the Earls of Lennox.

Visitors' moorings available. Bar & restaurant open Easter – Oct. (closed Tue.) Details/ferry - Tel: 01389 850245

Glen Fruin: "The Glen of Sorrow" remembers Colquhouns slaughtered at The Battle of Glen Fruin in 1603. The A817 winds its way towards Garelochhead, skirting the lower slopes of Shantron Hill, Balcnock, Beinn Tharsuinn and The Strone. A quieter alternative is the B832 .

Glen Finlas, west of the A82, is reached by a minor road from the A817 which dwindles to a path near Finlas Reservoir between dramatic, steep sided crags.

Rossdhu: ("Black Headland") is private parkland between the loch and the A82. The ruined castle (not accessible) was the home of the Chiefs of Clan Colquhoun until they built Rossdhu House, a beautiful Georgian stately mansion which currently houses the exclusive Loch Lomond Golf Club. The ornate gates to the estate can be seen from the A82.

Aldochlay: On a pedestal in a small bay is the tiny statue of "Wee Peter," thought to have been placed there in 1890 by stonemason William Kerr, who was born in Aldochlay.

Luss

In 510AD St. Kessog arrived from Ireland to preach Christianity. He founded a monastery on Inchtavannach. "Luss" may derive from the Gaelic "lus" meaning "herb" – St. Kessog was murdered and his body preserved in herbs which grew and covered his grave.

Later arrivals were not as peaceable or saintly: In the 13th century Vikings came via Loch Long, dragging their vessels

Luss

overland to Loch Lomond. In later years, the MacGregors, led by the infamous Rob Roy, regularly raided Luss. Inchlonaig, another island close to Luss, was planted with yew trees by Robert The Bruce to supply wood for his bowmen's weapons. In the 18th century Scottish towns were developing and slate quarries at Luss provided roof slates.

Today Luss is a delight. For over eight hundred years it has been at the heart of the Luss Estate, owned by the Colquhoun

Inchmurrin & Ben Lomond

family who continue to manage and nurture forty thousand acres of land. Parts of the village will be recognised as "Glendarroch" of TV's "Take The High Road." From the car park there are paths to the loch, with its sandy beach and views of Ben Lomond.

The Village Shop and Post Office sells everything for everyone – hot drinks, pies, cakes, tent pegs, bread , camping gas, dog food, postcards, fishing nets, wines and spirits, toiletries etc.

The Village Shop,Luss

The Farm Milk Bar serves hot and cold snacks, ice cream and hot soup. Open Easter – Oct.

Luss Glass Studio, in the old filling station, houses the work of talented glass artist Janine Smith. A former Glasgow

Luss Glass Blowing Studio

School of Art student, Janine's glass sculpted flowers are particularly striking.
Purdies at Luss: Coffees and teas, meals, visitor information.

Luss Village Walks: There are several signposted walks. An excellent National Parks leaflet details some, two of which are wheelchair and buggy friendly.

Luss Pier, built around 1845, was renovated and reopened in 1980 to serve the many boats which ply up and down the loch, including boat trips and the Loch Lomond Water Bus.

Luss Pier

Loch Lomond Leisure offer an imaginative choice of boat trips ranging from luxury speed boats to a pub tour on the water or an island BBQ. Also speedboat hire. Apr. – Oct. Other times by arrangement.
www.lochlomondscotland.com

The Loch Lomond Rescue Boat, founded in 1977, is manned by volunteers who work closely with the coastguard and National Park Authority.

<u>Luss Conservation Village</u>
Pier Street is lined with pretty cottages, built in the early 1800s to house quarry and mill workers and completely restored in the early 1990s. The cottages have narrow double doors typical of the time.

Old fashioned blooms such a hollyhocks complete the feeling of stepping back in time.

Cottages at Luss

Highland Arts has two branches in the village, selling high quality silver and pewter, tweeds, woollens, ladies' and gents' hats etc. A range of exclusive confectionary includes traditional butter tablet and truly delicious shortbread!

Highland Arts

The Coach House serves traditional Scottish food such as "stockies," haggis and clapshot plus home baking including stunning apple pie. Unusual tea pots feature in the adjacent gift shop. Dog friendly outside eating area. Open 10.00am. – 5.00pm. all year.

The Village Rest is a light airy café serving food and drinks all day. Open all year.
Play area – opposite The Village Rest is a children's playground with a rather friendly carved bear!
St. Kessog's Parish Church: St. Kessog founded the first church here over fifteen hundred years ago. The church contains fascinating relics: Graves include that of a Knight Templar and the hogback grave of a Viking prince. In 1314, after the Battle

St. Kessog's Parish Church

of Bannockburn, Robert The Bruce awarded land to the Earl of Lennox and charged him with care of the sacred site. During the Reformation some two hundred years later, a statue of the saint dating from around 1100AD along with the head of an older statue and an ancient font were hidden under a cairn at Bandry. They lay there until re-discovered in 1761 by soldiers building the military road along Loch Lomond. The three relics are in the church, which was built in 1875 by Sir James Colquhoun. The ceiling takes the form of an upturned boat in memory of Sir James' father who drowned in the loch.
The stained glass windows are beautiful; one commemorates the Rev. John Stuart

St. Kessog

who translated the Old Testament into Gaelic. The church welcomes visitors and the Sunday service from Luss is broadcast worldwide each week on the internet. **MacKessog Tartan**: In 2006 Luss further honoured St. Kessog by creating a special tartan, items of which are on sale at the Pilgrimage Centre.

Luss Pilgrimage and Information Centre: In 2011 Luss was awarded Green Pilgrimage City (!) status reflecting centuries of religious significance. The contemporary Pilgrimage Centre has a beautiful stone cross inlaid in the floor. There are various exhibitions and visitor information. Nearby is the Pilgrimage Path at The Glebe.

The Glebe: A small bridge, built in 2006 by The Royal Engineers, crosses Luss Water to a meadow dedicated to celebrating the concept of Pilgrimage. A beautiful Iona Cross is inset with Christian symbols including the Dove of Peace, grains of wheat, the candle of hope, symbols from other religions and the Luss Lily - a rare species which

Iona Cross, Luss

only grows here. Together the symbols spell out "co exist". Nearby trees were planted by HRH Prince Charles and Cardinal O'Brien. The picnic area was constructed by young people from various countries and is maintained by The Prince's Trust. In woodland near Luss live unusual white fallow deer whilst red deer frequent the higher ground.

The Loch Lomond Arms is a two hundred year old coaching inn. Notable visitors have included William and Dorothy Wordsworth in 1803. Recently restored to its former glory, the hotel offers a high standard of accommodation and seasonal dining.

Glen Luss, signposted from the A82, is a popular route with walkers wanting to scale Beinn Dubh or enjoy a gentler stroll along the track which follows Luss Water for a further two miles (3km).

The Lodge on Loch Lomond Hotel: The hotel's award winning restaurant, "Colquhoun's", overlooks the loch with decking for outside dining. Menus are extensive with imaginative side dishes.

The Camping and Caravanning Club Site, just north of Luss, enjoys a magnificent loch-side setting.

Loch Lomond Seaplanes: The ultimate Loch Lomond experience - a bird's eye

Loch Lomond Seaplanes

G-OLLS

(Picture courtesy of Loch Lomond Seaplanes)

view of amazing scenery and the thrill of taking off from and landing on the water in an iconic seaplane. Options include flying to Loch Lomond from Central Glasgow. The "Discovery Tour" takes passengers out towards the Mull of Kintyre, over the spectacular Arrochar Alps towards Mull, before overflying the Trossachs and finishing with a magnificent low level flight down the length of Loch Lomond. (Weather dependent). wwwlochlomondseaplanes.com

Inverbeg: Historically, cattle drovers used to cross the loch here - men in boats, cattle swimming behind.

The Inn at Inverbeg was originally a

The Inn at Inverbeg

droving inn. The present day hostelry is stylish. "Mr. C's Fish and Whisky Bar" offers dining in comfort. Open 10.00am for tea & coffee, midday until 9.00pm for food (9.30pm weekends.) Children's menu and takeaway food available.

Inverbeg Holiday Park, operated by Luss Estates, is a small, exclusive holiday park on a wooded peninsular with a private jetty.

Glen Douglas climbs steeply between Loch Lomond and Loch Long with spectacular views of Beinn Bhreac and Beinn Dubh.

Firkin Point is a lovely place with shore access, toilets and baby changing room. Here the loch is at its deepest – 200m (666'). There are easy walks along the old

Firkin Point

A82, now a cycle track/path. "Rubha" is Gaelic for "headland" and to the south is Rubha Mor while to the north is Rubha Dubh. Firkin Cottage was a toll house.

As the A82 carries on north, approaching Tarbet, it runs in the shadow of Ben Reoch, a popular climb with a stunning view from the summit over the Arrochar Alps to the north west.

Tarbet

Here, Loch Lomond and Loch Long are separated by less than two miles – "Tarbet" meaning a narrow strip of land over which boats could be carried. Viking raiders dragged their boats overland

Cruise Loch Lomond

between Loch long and Loch Lomond. Tarbet is another of the Highlands' major junctions: While the A82 runs the length of Loch Lomond, the A83 branches west to Arrochar, Inverary and the Argyll Forest. Tarbet makes a good place from which to explore by road, rail, bus or cruise boat. There is a large car park with public toilets, a jetty and a large, pleasant grassed picnic area.

Café Lochan is a small snack bar and information centre in the car park.

Cruise Loch Lomond offers cruises between Tarbet, Inversnaid, Luss, Balmaha and Rowardennan. All boats have toilets, bar facilities and are both dog and bike friendly. www.cruiselochlomond.co.uk Tel: 01301 702356

The Tarbet Hotel is a large, Baronial style building over two hundred and fifty years old, although there has been a hostelry on this site for over four hundred years. Many rooms overlook the loch and when Michael Portillo stayed here, on his epic rail tour for TV, he waxed eloquent about his "room with a loo with a view". Bar meals served Midday – 5.00pm.

VisitScotland, opposite the Tarbet Hotel, has a good selection of maps, guide books and gifts.

Tarbet Tea Rooms, open all year

10.00am – 5.00pm, serve a variety of meals and snacks, including particularly nice home-made scones! (Spot this sign!)

The Ballyhennan Restaurant is in a converted church on the Arrochar road. Open Mon. – Fri. from 5.00pm. Sat. – Sun. from 3.00pm.

Toilets
Luss – either end of the village centre car park and by the pier
Firkin Point
The car park, Tarbet.
Internet Access
The phone box in Luss car park

3. WESTERN LOCH LOMOND: TARBET TO TYNDRUM

North of Tarbet, the road clings to the loch shore , twisting and turning amongst the trees with glimpses of the railway high above the road. (See map on page 9).

Western Loch Lomond

"On the bonnie, bonnie banks of Loch Lomond....."

hill into a graceful building, the generating plant of the Loch Sloy Hydro Scheme, built in the mid 1940s and opened by the then Queen in 1950. During the day, water is carried three miles from Loch Sloy and rushes down the pipes to turn the turbines. At night water is pumped back up to Loch Sloy.

Inveruglas Power Station

The Bonnie Braes was originally a croft house dating from 1740. This informal restaurant serves local fresh produce all year round. Sit in or out.
Loch Lomond Holiday and Caravan Park, set in woodland on the banks of the loch, has its own private bay and is a great place to stay, especially for boating.

Inveruglas has a car park, information centre, small cafe and a jetty for loch cruises or the ferry to Inversnaid (seasonal). A viewpoint and picnic site overlook Inveruglas Isle. On the island are the ruins of a castle, once home to the Chief of Clan MacFarlane, but destroyed by Roundheads in the 17th century.
A series of gigantic pipes run down the

Loch Lomond from Inveruglas

Pulpit Rock, north of the traffic lights on a narrow bend, is a huge boulder with a window shaped hollow. Two tales tell its history: Before 1825 it was known as "Clach nan Tarbh" ("stone of the bulls") from a Celtic legend of two huge bulls who lived on either side of the loch who roared at each other across the water. One day the eastern bull came round the top of the loch and down Glen Falloch. The two fought so ferociously that the noise brought the boulder tumbling down from the mountain top. Many centuries later the rock gained its present name: Until the early 19th century, people from Ardlui travelled seven miles (11km) to Arrochar each Sunday to worship. In 1817, they begged the new minister to come and preach there too. He agreed if they would build him a pulpit. The hollow was blasted in the boulder to provide a shelter and a wooden pulpit constructed in front. It was used until 1895 when the Ardlui Mission Church was opened.

Ardlui

Ardlui is at the northern tip of the loch, where it is joined by the River Falloch. Its name derives from the Gaelic "height of the calves", perhaps referring to the custom of moving cattle to higher grazing land for the summer. Above Ardlui are the remains of several "sheilings" (summer shelters).

Ardlui Station opened in 1894 and is familiar to rail passengers as the place to stretch ones legs until the train from the opposite direction arrives at the passing loop. Nearby is one of the starting points for the ascent of 943m (3093') high Ben Vorlich.

The Ardlui Hotel and Caravan Site enjoys a superb loch-side position.

Open all year, meals are available all day, every day. Accommodation includes a hotel as well as camping, caravans, log cabins, camping pods etc. The hotel ferry runs between Ardlui and Ardleish Farm from Apr. to Oct. (other times by

The Ardlui Hotel

arrangement). At the side of the hotel is a shop selling a range of foodstuffs, maps, guide books, fishing permits etc.

Ardlui Marina offers full facilities for boating visitors – moorings, pontoons, hoist, slipway, fuel and pump out station.

Inverarnan

Inverarnan sits on the old Loch Lomond drove route. Trading reached its peak during the 17th century. Drovers travelled the Highlands and Islands buying cattle for markets in the Scottish Lowlands and England. Over thirty thousand cattle crossed the border each year.

The Drovers Inn is a must! Over three

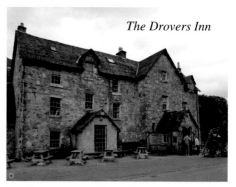

The Drovers Inn

hundred years old and once called The Inverarnan Inn, it is a quirky place:

The building is a maze of nooks and crannies, stags' heads and other tributes to the art of taxidermy. The inn is said to be haunted. There is a varied menu and a good range of beers and whiskies. The annex across the road offers comfortable, modern rooms.

The Drovers Inn

North of Ardlui is evidence of a section of the River Falloch being converted into a canal in the mid 1800s by a landowner who operated a steamer on the loch. The canal was used for over fifteen years until a pier was built at Ardlui.

Beinglas Farm Camp Site nestles on the West Highland Way below Ben Glas. The camp site also has wigwams, chalets, a restaurant, bar and small shop.

Grey Mares Tail Waterfall is a quarter of a mile (0.4km) up the Ben Glas Burn from Beinglas Farm.

Glen Falloch

"Falach" is Gaelic for "hiding place". Between Crianlarich and Loch Lomond the A82 passes between high, rocky peaks. Robert The Bruce then Rob Roy MacGregor both sought refuge here. The road crosses many burns tumbling down to join the River Falloch which has carved a deep route between the rocks and boulders of the glen floor.

The Falls of Falloch are signposted from the road. A pleasant woodland path meanders above the river for a quarter of a mile (0.4km) to the waterfall. Legend decrees that Rob Roy took time to swim when he passed this way.

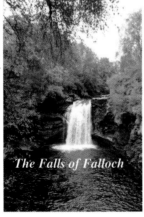

The Falls of Falloch

Crianlarich

"A' Chrion Láraich" is Gaelic for "the low pass". The village is overlooked from the east by towering Ben More. After the 1745 Jacobite uprising, General Wade established a Scottish road system for troops to travel quickly to quell Highland unrest. Crianlarich developed where two such roads met. A century and a half later two railways met here – the Oban to Callander Line and The West Highland Line. The village then had four signal boxes and two stations. The sidings and thirteen-bay engine shed, now a Scheduled Grade C Building, remain although the Callander line closed in 1965. Trains from Glasgow split here for the onward journey, to either Fort William or Oban. Crianlarich is also a busy road junction where the A85 meets the A82.

The Station Tea Rooms: The original station was unusual for its time in that it had a dining room. The present building replaced one which burned down in 1962. Enjoy a drink or meal right on the station platform - or grab a slice of home-made cake to take with you. Open 7.30am. – 4.00pm. (seasonal)

The Crianlarich Hotel was originally a

The Crianlarich Hotel

droving inn. It is reputed to have been one of Rob Roy's haunts. The present building dates from the early 19th century and has been tastefully refurbished to combine "olde worlde" charm with modern facilities. It is a warm, welcoming place, serving food all day between 7.30am and 9.30pm from breakfast, to tea and cakes, award winning bar meals or a full restaurant menu. (Look out for a wily fox in the bar!)

pleasant half mile (0.8km) stroll in Forestry Commission land – a good place for a journey break with young, fidgety travellers! Nearby is a playground.

A wily fox!

Well: Set in a wall just north of the hotel is an intriguing well or shrine.

War Memorial: The attractive sandstone war memorial at the A82/A85 junction was erected in 1922 by Alexander Carrick who also created the one at Killin. The statue is of a soldier of The Black Watch Regiment.

Granite Memorial: A granite memorial in the middle of the village remembers three men who lost their lives when a plane on a test flight flew into Ben More.

Crianlarich Store is a well stocked post office and mini supermarket, also selling teas and coffees, hot snacks and much more. There is also a cash machine.

Crianlarich Youth Hostel is spacious and modern.

Crianlarich Community Woodland is a

Crianlarich Church, especially pretty, was designed by architect Thomas Ross and built in 1901.

The Rod and Reel serve good value, traditional pub grub. This is the place to find "a chunk of steak pie" – large, home-made pies cut into portions. (Recommended by Lynne's Dad!) It is

The Rod & Reel, Crianlarich

also the place to obtain fishing permits for the River Fillan, have your West Highland Way logbook stamped or take your dog for a pint in a pet friendly bar. Open 11am – 11pm. Mar. - Oct.

Ben More Lodge Hotel has self catering lodges and welcomes touring caravans and motor homes. The fully licensed restaurant serves breakfasts as well as snacks, bar meals, dinner and packed lunches. The bar has a good selection of ales and malt whiskies and a roaring log fire on cooler days. Free Wi-fi.

Strathfillan

Strath is the Scottish name for a wide, shallow valley such as Strathfillan which runs between Tyndrum and Crianlarich to Loch Dochart. St. Fillan's Priory, the remains of which can still be seen, was founded in the 14th century by Robert The Bruce. (See below.)

St Fillan's Priory & The Holy Pool. At Kirkton a minor road from the A82 crosses the River Fillan to Kirkton Farm. Nearby are the remains of the priory and pool.

Strathfillan Wigwams, at Auchtertyre, is a working farm and a superb camp site

Strathfillan Wigwams

with facilities for family holidays, day visitors and intrepid souls passing through on the West Highland Way. There are toilets, showers, internet access and a cookhouse. The farm shop sells camping and walking essentials, coffee and bacon rolls. (For a treat, there are nice preserves and pâtés too!) There are riverside and woodland walks, a sheep trail and access

to Kirkton (see above). Higher treks beginning here include Ben Challuim, Beinn Odhar and Beinn Chaorach.

Dalrigh

Tyndrum Community Woodland, south of Tyndrum and signposted "Dalrigh," is part of the Caledonian Forest with ancient

pines. Walks from the car park include following the Crom Allt Burn through an area of drumlins (glacial mounds). In the woods is an old lead smelting site. Recently, gold and silver have also been found in this area, although not for the first time: Sir Robert Clifton mined for lead and gold during the 18th century and there was a gold mine at nearby Cononish.

The Battle of Dalrigh: (1306) Robert The Bruce was pursued here by John MacDougall of Lorne. Robert's men threw their heaviest weapons into a lochan as they tried to flee. According to legend, Robert's sword remains at the bottom of the pool.

Tyndrum

Here, several routes converge: North is Glen Coe and Fort William; west is Oban;

south is Crianlarich, Loch Lomond and Callander. The West Highland Way passes through the village, as does the Oban to St. Andrews Coast to Coast Walk. Since the days of cattle drovers, Tyndrum has catered for weary travellers, as it does today.

Railway Stations: There are two stations – Upper Tyndrum on the Fort William line and Lower Tyndrum on the track to Oban.

The Green Welly Stop is a family-run establishment catering for all visitors' needs. The restaurant serves home-made Scottish food, a speciality being Cullen

The Green Welly Stop

Skink. The Snack Stop Café serves lighter meals, takeaways and home-made pizzas until 9.00pm. The Outdoor Store stocks clothing, maps, guide books, walking poles etc. There are excellent gift shops and The Whisky Shop. The toilets deserve a special mention as they are invariably spotless. Also - a filling Station for fuel.

VisitScotland has a large information centre in the middle of the village.

Paddy's Rock 'n Roll Diner at Tyndrum Lodge Hotel is a wonderfully quirky place with seats like beer bottle tops, a full sized Elvis, a giant beefburger and an amazing menu. Open all year 7.30am – midnight.

Paddy's Rock 'n Roll Diner

The Real Food Café is a true gem – fast food for real foodies! Beefburgers are 100% Scottish beef, eggs are free range, haddock suppers use fish landed at Fort William, the stove burns real logs and the venison pie and apple crumble, as with everything else, are home made. Open Mon. to Thu.11.30am – 9.00pm, Sat. from 9.00am. Sun. from 10.00am. Weekends only in Winter.

Brodie's Minimarket is a small convenience store.

By The Way Hostel and Camp Site is just off the main road on the West Highland Way. Backpackers and walkers are catered for with an indoor camping kitchen, tent drying room, bike shelter, trekker huts and a shop selling sustenance

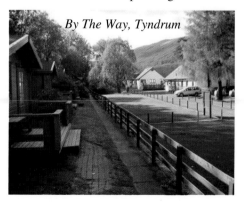

By The Way, Tyndrum

for body and sole (!) – "blister ointments, plasters, bandages and sympathy!"

Forestry Commission Walks: From Lower Tyndrum Station there are several signposted.

Pine Trees Leisure Park: Caravans, tents and trekkers' huts; showers, laundry, microwave and TV. Child/pet friendly. Calor Gas stockist. Open Mar. - Oct.

By yon bonnie banks,
And by yon bonnie braes......

(Old Scottish Song, Copyright Unknown.)

Public Toilets
The car park, Tarbet.
Crianlarich
Strathfillan Wigwams
Tyndrum, main road
The Green Welly Stop, Tyndrum.
Internet Access
Ben More Lodge, Crianlarich (Wi-Fi)
Crianlarich Youth Hostel
(available to non residents)
Strathfillan Wigwams, Auchtertrye
Tyndrum Internet Café, Community Centre. Tues. and Fri. 11.00 am. – 4pm.

4. EASTERN LOCH LOMOND: BALLOCH TO ROWARDENNAN

Eastern Loch Lomond

The eastern shore has no continuous road along its length. From Drymen, the B837 joins the loch at Balmaha to run the 6.8 miles (11km) to Rowardennan. The road ends there, although the well trodden path of the West Highland Way continues to the northern tip of the loch, passing through Inversnaid, the only other place with road access - a 15 miles (24km) road from Aberfoyle, along the shores of Lochs Chon, Ard and Arklet.

Balloch to Drymen
The A811 between Balloch and Drymen enjoys panoramic views of the distant hills on the far side of the loch to the west.

The Loch Lomond Bird of Prey Centre is committed to education and bird rescue and has a picnic area, small shop and lots of information. The website has a first aid section on injured birds. Wheelchair accessible but cannot admit guide dogs. www.lochlomondbirdofpreycentre.co.uk

Loch Lomond Homes & Gardens Centre, adjacent to the Bird of Prey Centre, has a large selection of garden furniture and equipment, plants and gifts, Café and children's play area.

Gartocharn
Meaning "place of the humped hill," this was once the home of Scottish climber, author and broadcaster Tom Weir, remembered for the TV series "Weir's Way."

23

EASTERN LOCH LOMOND

1 Bird of Prey Centre
2 The Dumpling
3 The House of Darroch
4 Kilmaranock Church
5 Buchanan Parish church
6 Inchmurrin
7 Inchcailloch
8 Cashel Forest
9 Ross Point
10 Ben Lomond National Memorial Park
11 Hotel
12 Youth Hostel
13 Doug Cocker sculpture
14 Ben View Garden Centre
15 Robert Bontine Cunningham Graham Monument
16 Gartmore House

25 Go Country
26 Loch Arklet Dam
27 Bunk House & Bistro
28 Rob Roy's View
29 Craigroyston Woods
30 Inversnaid Hotel
31 RSPB Reserve
32 Rob Roy's Cave

STRONACHLACHAR
Loch Cruises
Pier Tea Rooms
Boat & cycle hire
Fishing

P - car park

ABERFOYLE
Scottish Wool Centre
VisitScotland Information
The Poker Tree
St. Mary's Episcopal Church
Aberfoyle Parish Church

BALMAHA
National Park Visitor Centre
Oak Tree Inn
Craigie Fort
Boat Hire

DRYMEN
War Memorial
The Clachan Inn
The Rob Roy Way
Steak & Mealy Pie
Ealain Gallery
Body & Beauty
Viewpoint
Lomond Activities
Buchanan Castle
Golf clubs

17 Gartartan Castle
18 Mile post
19 Aberfoyle Golf Course
20 Kirkton Burial Ground
21 The Duke's Pass
22 Forest trails & sculptures
23 Wee Blether
24 Great Times Scotland

Aberfoyl
Gartmore
Stronachlachar
Ben Venue
Kinlochard
Kirkton
Loch Katrine
B829
L. Chon
L.Dhu
Ben L. Ard
Rowardennan
Inversnaid
L. Arklet
Ben Lomond
Balmaha
Buchanan Smithy
Drymen
Gartocharm
Endrick Water
A81
A809
A811
Loch Lomond
Balloch
N

24

Gartocharn is a pretty village nestling beneath Duncryne, a conical hill also known as "The Dumpling." Gartocharn has some attractive houses and a quaint old petrol pump.

Gartocharn

Kilmaranock Church

The House of Darroch is a retail outlet selling quality clothing & accessories, gifts and Scottish foods, including a range of speciality cured bacons and meats. There is a coffee shop and restaurant – a special treat being afternoon tea with smoked salmon and champagne!

The House of Darroch

A children's playground can be found just beyond Darroch House.

Duncryne Equitation & Trekking Centre caters for all standards of riders. Trekking all year round in spectacular scenery. Tel: 01389 830425

Kilmaranock Church graveyard has a number of ornate tombstones bearing carved urns with stone drapes. Fashionable in Victorian times, the urn is a classical symbol of mourning, representing the body as the vessel for the soul. The drape represents death. Tom Weir (see page 23) was buried here in 2006.

Draped Urn

Endrick Water:
The A811 is carried over the river by a graceful, five-arched, sandstone bridge, near the A809 junction. The original 1765 bridge was widened and reinforced with concrete in the early 20th century.

Drymen.
Four miles (6.5km) from Loch Lomond, Drymen (pronounced "Drimmen" and meaning "on the ridge") was once a major droving centre with two annual cattle fairs and a weekly market. The village has many associations with Rob Roy's long standing feud with the Duke of Montrose. A walking guide is available from the library.

The War Memorial, a simple granite cross, has a moving inscription, reminding us that wars were fought so we could all live in freedom.

Drymen

The **Clachan Inn**, dating from 1734, is Scotland's oldest licensed pub. It serves excellent food with a full menu as well as lighter meals.

The Rob Roy Way is the 79 mile

The Clachan Inn

(127km) long-distance path between Drymen and Pitlochry. The official start point is at the doorstep of the Clachan Inn.

The West Highland Way also passes through the village, as does Route 7 of the National Cycle Network between Land's End and John O' Groats.

The Village Shop & Post Office, as well as being extremely helpful, sells newspapers, books, maps and other essentials such as blister plasters etc.

The Convenience Store in the village is well stocked with groceries etc.

David MacDonald Butchers: For

something out of the ordinary try the unique, award-winning Steak and Mealy Pie (steak, sausage and white pudding)!

The Hawthorns is an imposing house built in 1873 by the Duke of Montrose to attract a doctor to the village. It is now a pleasant B and B, the kitchen occupying the former surgery. It has the distinction of having been one of the first concrete houses in Scotland.

The Winnock Hotel dates partly from the 1700s and was once four separate thatched cottages, one being an alehouse. It is a friendly place with a choice of dining options and also hosts regular Ceilidhs and Scottish Nights - national music from bagpipes to Scottish opera.

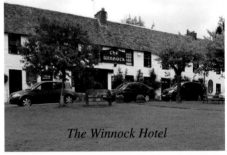

The Winnock Hotel

Drymen Pottery, no longer a working pottery, is an unusual place to dine - a choice of coffee shop, restaurant, outside conservatory or terrace dining – and a pub upstairs! Open 9.30am – 9.00pm weekdays, Sun. from 10.00am. Shorter hours in winter.

Ealain Gallery: "Ealain" is Gaelic for "art." The gallery features original works by contemporary Scottish artists, also ceramics and giftware. Open daily.

The Whisky Cellar at Ealain Gallery holds daily malt whisky tastings.

The Buchanan Arms is a large hotel with a health and leisure club including spa and swimming pool. The Salmon Leap Restaurant serves traditional Scottish dishes as well as international cuisine. Lighter dishes also available between 12.00 noon and 5.00pm.

The Buchanan Arms

Fourth Duke of Montrose in 1855 after Buchanan House burned down. After his death in 1925 it was a hotel and then a WWII military hospital – one famous inmate being Rudolph Hess injured during his infamous parachute jump.

Buchanan Castle

Golf: Drymen can boast two golf clubs – Strathendrick and Buchanan Castle.

Body and Beauty by Maxine – for that holiday pamper! Situated on the main street, treatments include manicure, pedicure, aromatherapy, reflexology, Swedish massage. Tel: 07713 400216.

Loch Viewpoint: From opposite the Buchanan Arms a path leads to a viewpoint over Loch Lomond. Several islands can be seen as well as the hills on the opposite shore.

Lomond Activities have bikes for hire (all year.) Tel: 01360 660066

The Church of Scotland, on the southern side of the village, is an imposing white painted building dating from 1771.

Buchanan Castle, near Buchanan Castle Golf Club, looks like something from a fairy tale – still standing to full height and complete with turrets, it is almost totally cloaked in foliage. Originally Buchanan land, the estate was sold to the Montrose family in 1682. The castle was built by the

Drymen to Rowardennan

From Drymen, the B837 leads to Loch Lomond's eastern shore, passing through some interesting hamlets and villages.

Buchanan Smithy (Smiddy) is a row of pretty, early 19th century white cottages, built by the Duke of Montrose to house estate workers. The original smithy

Buchanan "Smiddy"

building can still be seen.

Milton of Buchanan: "Milton" affixed to place-names denotes either "middle" or "a place with a mill", in this case the latter: The mill, now a private house, remains - with the water wheel fully restored.

Buchanan Parish Church is a pretty building. The central porch has a small bell tower ("bellcote"). It was designed by John Adam (1721 – 1792.) In the churchyard is a sundial commemorating a

Buchanan Parish Church

minister who served here for thirty years. Nearby is the stone of Charles MacPhie (1813 – 1890) who was schoolmaster for forty-two years. Military gravestones include those of servicemen who died at Buchanan Castle military hospital. An imposing, but more recent, stone is that of Lord Bannerman of Kildonnan.

Balmaha

"Balmaha" derives either from the Gaelic "St. Maha's Place" or from "Bal Maitheas" – a church offering refuge. Today, it is the boating centre for the eastern side of the loch, as well as being on the West Highland Way. Balmaha gets very busy in summer and it is advisable to park at the large car park at the National Park Visitor Centre.

The National Park Visitor Centre is excellent. Information about the loch and local flora and fauna includes displays about The Highland Boundary Fault. The centre stands out for its child friendly atmosphere – things to pick up and touch with comfy seats for waiting adults!

National Park Visitor Centre, Balmaha

There are several walks from the car park, one to the top of Conic Hill, a less strenuous one to Craigie Fort and the one mile (1.6km) Millennium Forest Trail. Look out for red squirrels who enjoy the beech nuts here. The nearby play area features a willow maze.

Red squirrel

Craigie Fort is the remains of a prehistoric defensive walled settlement on top of Craigie Hill. The steep ridge to one side provided a natural defence. The views of Ben Lomond and the Arrochar Alps make the climb worthwhile!

The Village Shop: Taking the view that "some come for a day, some come for a week" this shop has it all; groceries, chilled meats, newspapers, wines & spirits and wonderful vacuum packed smoked fish from the inn next door. Fresh coffee available, also a cash machine. Open 7.00am – 10.00pm. (Shorter hours in winter.)

The Village Shop, Balmaha

Balmaha Bunkhouse offers reasonably priced accommodation, B and B or bunkhouse, in a spectacular setting right on Balmaha Bay.

Balmaha Bay

The Oak Tree Inn is family-owned and serves Scottish ales and malt whiskies, including the most local one - Glengoyne, a ten year old malt. On the menu is locally sourced food, including home smoked fish and cloutie dumpling made from a secret family recipe (a traditional pudding made with suet, flour, dried fruit and spices).

The Loch Lomond Water Bus departs from a pier at the far end of the bay (summer only).

The Oak Tree Inn

Loch Lomond Water Bus

Macfarlane & Son is one of the oldest boatyards on the loch, operating the mail boat to the islands, cruises to Inchcailloch Nature Trail (see below) and a range of other cruises. Also boat hire and fishing permits. Tel: 01360 870214.

Balmaha Bay has jetties for the many pleasure craft usually moored here and looks across to Inchcailloch only a few hundred yards away.

Inchcailloch, "island of the old woman" or "island of nuns," is one of only three islands on the loch not privately owned, this one in the care of the National Park Authority and Scottish Natural Heritage. St. Kentigena arrived here in AD717. A church dedicated to her was built around the early 13th century. Local people rowed across to worship here until a church was built on the mainland in 1670.

At one time there was a factory producing lignin for tanning at Balmaha. Oaks to supply bark used in the process were grown on Inchcailloch. The factory closed in 1920. Today, tree-creepers thrive on the insects they find in the tree bark and woodpeckers can often be heard. Inchcailloch is uninhabited and forms part of the Loch Lomond National Nature Reserve. Tom na Nighranan, the island's highest point, has wonderful views including Ben Lomond. The island is renowned for its crop of bluebells. It is accessible by boat from Macfarlane & Son (see page 29). There are wooden piers for private boats at either end of the island. Camping on the island can be booked through the National Park Authority.

Inchmurrin is a pleasant trip from Balmaha on the mail boat. On the island is a hotel serving morning coffee, lunch and dinner. See page 10 for details.

Beyond Balmaha the road runs alternately next to the shore and through mixed woodland. Oaks here were planted by the Third Duke of Montrose in the 18th century. No stopping or parking is allowed other than in designated places for this six mile (9.6km) stretch of road.

Milarrochy Bay

Milarrochy Bay is a pretty bay with a National Park Ranger base, car park, toilets and boat launching facilities. Thirsty canine tourists can usually find a drinking bowl by the Ranger base.

National Park Ranger Base

Milarrochy Bay Camping and Caravanning Club Site also has backpacker facilities for drying, washing and cooking (no pre booking required) as well as a shop selling groceries etc.

Cashel Forest, one of Scotland's Millennium Forest Projects, has an interpretive centre containing information about the trees and the many species of butterflies, dragonflies and birds to be found locally. There is also a beautiful carving of an oak tree, fashioned from a piece of bark. Nearby is a picnic area and group barbeque facilities. Different walks cater for varying fitness levels with viewpoints, cairns and wood sculptures along the way. Leaflets are available from a dispenser by the notice board. www.cashel.org.uk

Strathcashell Point: Opposite the entrance to Cashel Forest a footpath leads to the site of an Iron Age fort.

Cashel Caravan Park & Campsite: "Camping in the Forest" is a partnership between the Camping and Caravanning Club and The Forestry Commission. Excellent facilities include a laundry, take-away, shop and loch access for boat launching.

Sallochy Woodland Camping: Another woodland camp site on the loch shore, this is a wonderful place to cook a meal over an open fire (mobile fire pits available). Booking is essential through Forestry Commission Scotland. (No outdoor consumption of alcohol allowed). Trees from Sallochy were sent as timber for ships in the navy of James IV, floated down to Dumbarton shipyards.

Ross Point: Less than a mile (1.6km) north of Sallochy is a picnic site, from which it is possible to follow the West Highland Way for a short distance then branch left onto a track through Ross Wood towards Ross Point. Capercaille are said to live in these woods.

Rowardennan

The public road ends at Rowardennan, nestling beneath Ben Lomond. From here The West Highland Way continues north and a ferry crosses the loch from here (Apr. – Sep). There is a hotel, Youth Hostel, small pier and access to The Ben Lomond National Memorial Park.

The Rowardennan Hotel offers hotel rooms, lodges or bunk rooms but also caters for non residents who arrive by car, boat or on foot. There is a warm welcome for everyone in The Clansman Bar,

including dogs and dirty boots! The view from the beer garden defies adequate description. Reasonably priced food is served from 11.00am, including a take-away menu.

Rowardennan

The Ben Lomond National Memorial Park is the most popular starting point for the ascent of The Ben. Car parking is limited and it gets busy. Ben Lomond, at

974m (3195') is Scotland's most southerly Munro (mountain over 3000') and one of

Sallochy

the most popular, some thirty thousand people climbing it each year. The park includes the summit and surrounding area

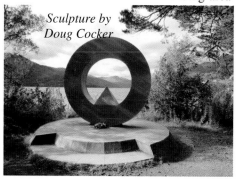

Sculpture by Doug Cocker

down to the shore and is a designated War Memorial to those who gave their lives in the two World Wars. In the car park is an information point. A short distance from the car park is an evocative sculpture by Doug Cocker – representing a rifle sight which perfectly frames the view up the loch. From here it is possible to follow part of The West Highland Way along the shore.

Ardess Hidden History Trail is a low level trail past ruined settlements (leaflet available at the start of the trail).

Rob Roy's Cave, some two and a half miles (4km) along the Rob Roy Way to

the north of the hotel, was a place of hiding also reputed to have been used four centuries earlier by Robert The Bruce after The Battle of Dalrigh. (see page 21).

The National Trust for Scotland Rangers' Office is along the private road beyond the car park.

Ranger vehicle

Public Toilets
The Winnock Hotel, Drymen
Visitor Centre Balamha
Milarrochy Bay
Cashel Forest Centre
Car park, Ben Lomond National
Memorial Park

Internet Access
National Park Visitor Centre, Balmaha

5. E. LOMOND: DRYMEN, ABERFOYLE, INVERSNAID

Drymen to Aberfoyle

The A811 follows the old Dumbarton to Stirling military road with views to the south east of the Campsie Fells. The A81 Aberfoyle road branches north from the A811.

Ben View Garden Centre, three miles (4.8km) north of the junction, is an excellent place to stop for a coffee, browse the garden and antique centre and admire the spectacular display of blooms

in the orchid house. Open daily from 9.00am (10.30am Sun.)

The Trossachs Holiday Park, further along the A81, is an award winning camping and caravan site.

Gartmore

This delightful village, on one of the old drove routes and a short detour from the A81, is an example of a planned estate village. "Gart mòr" translates as "large field" or "cattle enclosure". It was during the 18th century that the village developed into its present form on the Gartartan Estate, owned by the Graham family until the beginning of the 20th century. Sir Charles Cayzer then made further improvements. The village sits on a ridge and on a clear day it is possible to see the Wallace Monument 25 miles (40km) away at Stirling. In 2004 an earthquake (4.5 on the Richter scale) shook the village, which lies very near the Highland Boundary Fault. The Rob Roy Way passes through the village. In 1753 at Gartmore Fair Rob Og, son of Rob Roy, was arrested and subsequently hanged for the abduction and forced marriage of a widow.

The War Memorial is in the centre of the village near some information boards detailing the history of Gartmore.

A children's play area is near the War Memorial.

The Village Shop and Post Office is a grocery store, off licence and newsagents.

The Black Bull: Built in the early 18th century, the inn was popular with cattle drovers, including Rob Roy. Accommodation available and food served all day.

Gartmore Parish Church was built in 1790 and extended in 1904. It has a pretty bellcote as well as attractive wrought iron gates. A moon dial, formerly at Gartmore House, sits in the Cayzer family burial ground (private land) behind the building.

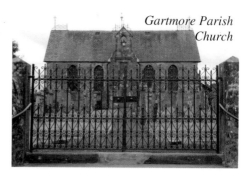

Gartmore Parish Church

The Robert Bontine Cunningham Graham Monument overlooks the playing field. A famous writer, traveller and political leader, he was born in 1852. He went to Argentina as a horse and cattle dealer, becoming known as "Don Roberto". He later inherited the Gartmore Estate and became an MP. He was imprisoned for joining the free speech riots of 1889 and later become the first leader of the National Party of Scotland (later the SNP). He died in Argentina in 1936. His remains are buried on Inchmahome on the Lake of Menteith.

Monument, Gartmore

Gartmore House is a beautiful Baronial house, built in 1793 by William Adam and owned by the Graham family until the early 20th century. It was bought by Sir Charles Cayzer and remodelled by David Barclay, a student of Charles Rennie Mackintosh. There is a lovely old sundial in front of the main entrance. The house is now a Christian conference centre. Visitors are welcome to wander through the grounds.

Gartartan Castle, in the grounds of Gartmore House, is the ruin of a 16th century "Z-plan" tower.

Milepost: Opposite Gartartan Lodge is a beautiful old painted milepost, one of several along this road.

Action Adventure Activities, at Easterhill Farm, offers exciting outdoor pursuits including sphering/zorbing (rolling down hill inside a giant ball!) Pre booked visits only.

Aberfoyle

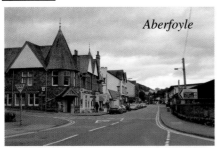

Aberfoyle

This is a lively village on the banks of the River Forth, within the Queen Elizabeth Forest Park. It is the southern gateway to The Trossachs and the only route to Inversnaid. Aberfoyle rapidly became a fashionable tourist destination after 1810 when Sir Walter Scott published his epic poem "The Lady of The Lake", set around Loch Katrine.

In 1882 the railway arrived to bring tourists and carry away slate for a thriving industry which reached its peak during the 19th century. During the 1930s the quarry provided slate for the billiard tables on board The Queen Mary. A narrow gauge railway ran down the hill to the railway yard, now the car park. The quarry closed in 1958.

Aberfoyle is a popular centre with a bank, post office, supermarket, restaurants, police station and a range of hotels and guest houses. There is a large car park with bicycle racks in the centre of the village. The Rob Roy Way passes through Aberfoyle and there are several way-marked paths and cycle trails from the centre of the village, some along the old railway which is suitable for wheelchairs etc. One of Aberfoyle's notable inhabitants was the Reverend Robert Kirk. (see page 35).

The Rob Roy Hotel sits at the A81/A821 junction and offers accommodation, reasonably priced food all day in the Thistle Bar and lunch and dinner in the Tartan Room.

Aberfoyle Golf Club (18 holes) is at the eastern end of the village.

The Scottish Wool Centre features outdoor animal shows, including a clever sheepdog who herds ducks over a series of obstacles! (Apr. – Sept. Free.) There is also a food and whisky hall, knitwear and a restaurant.

The VisitScotland Trossachs Discovery Centre is on the main car park. A leaflet of walks from Aberfoyle is available.

The Poker Tree, at the west of the village, is an oak tree in which hangs a large, red poker to commemorate one used by Bailie Nichol Jarvie in a fight at the

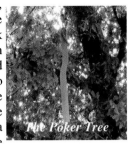

The Poker Tree

Aberfoyle Inn in Scott's "Rob Roy" novel. An information board in the car park tells the tale.

The choice of places to eat in Aberfoyle is too great to mention all:

The Coach House is a family friendly restaurant and bar serving food all day.

The Clachan Lounge Bar is an interesting and inexpensive place to eat. A plate of traditional Haggis, Neeps and Tatties is exceptionally good value. The

walls are covered in various intriguing collections, including old cameras.

Liz MacGreggor's licensed restaurant and coffee shop offers excellent value for wholesome cooking and baking. (The

children's menu includes real food!) Eat in or collect goodies for a picnic. The cakes are irresistible and the soup is delicious.

The Forth Inn is popular, centrally situated and serves several real ales and over fifty malt whiskies in The Wallace Bar. Breakfasts available between 9.00am and 11.00am. Open all year.

The Forth Inn

The Post Office is friendly, helpful and stocks stationery, maps, books and fishing

The Reverend Robert Kirk was a 17th century minister, reputedly the seventh son of a seventh son and thought to have supernatural powers. He became famous for his belief in fairies and the mysterious circumstances surrounding his death. In 1691 he published a book entitled *"The Secret Commonwealth of Elves, Fauns & Faeries"*. He believed that Doune Hill at Aberfoyle was inhabited by spirits and in May 1692 is supposed to have had his soul imprisoned in a pine tree as reprisal for publishing fairy secrets. He was found dead, dressed only in his nightshirt, and is buried in Kirkton Graveyard. A lone Scots Pine can still be seen on top of the hill, guarding the Fairy Queen's underground palace, sometimes with ribbons attached in memory of Rev. Robert Kirk.

permits.

The Wee Tablet Shop sells Amy Johnson's famous Scottish tablet and other sweets.

Rainbow's End is a gift shop and newsagents with an upstairs tea room. Open all year.

Guyana Garden Centre stocks gifts from all over the World, plants and gardening items.

The Wee Market sells antiques & curios.

"Chillout" is the place for a relaxing holistic therapy or a tasteful gift. Booking: 01877 389302.

St. Mary's Episcopal Church is a beautiful building with a pretty bellcote. It was built in 1893 by quarrymen who laboured for free on their days off. Many

St. Mary's Episcopal Church

of the present congregation are their direct descendents. The church is of a simple Gothic Arts and Crafts style, designed by James Miller (1860 – 1947) who also designed The Gleneagles Hotel and Stirling Railway Station. The church has an unusual hammer beamed roof. The oak font cover features a carved squirrel and bird. On one wall hangs a painting of the quarry as it would have looked in 1900. This was executed by Moira Revie

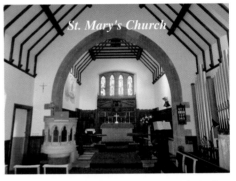

St. Mary's Church

on a piece of slate. From behind the church, paths lead into the woodland. Service: Sun. 11.15am.

Aberfoyle "New" Parish Church (Church of Scotland) was built in 1870 to replace the Old Kirk on the other side of the river. It was designed in early Gothic style by John Honeyman and enlarged in 1884. The elegant interior contains lovely 19th century stained glass windows and one from 1974 by Gordon Webster. Coloured Minton tiles floor the sanctuary. A bell, dating from 1725 and presented to the old church by The Duke of Montrose, hangs from a stone frame. In front of the church stands the War Memorial. Service: Sun. 11.15am.

Kirkton: A minor road leads over a

humped back bridge to Kirkton, site of the original village and the former parish church where the Reverend Robert Kirk, "The Faerie Minister", is buried. The church, now in ruins, was built in 1744 but abandoned in 1870 when the new church was built. The graveyard has two cast iron "mort safe" coffins - too heavy for grave robbers to carry!

From the western end of the village the A821 turns sharply up hill towards Duke's Pass, the eastern end of Loch Katrine and on to Callander (see page 53) while the B829 goes to the western end of Loch Katrine and Inversnaid.

Aberfoyle to Stronachlachar and Inversnaid. (B829)

You are now following in royal footsteps! On October 14th 1859 Queen Victoria officially opened the Loch Katrine water system (see page 40). Black and white painted cast iron mileposts mark the way - in place since Queen Victoria's visit. The narrow B829 road is especially picturesque. Just west of Aberfoyle by the junction to Milton is a former corn mill, the remains of the iron waterwheel still visible.

Loch Ard Forest (Milton Car Park):

The forest covers some 37 square miles (10,000 hectares) and includes several lochs, a forest drive for cars, a bridleway (with parking for horseboxes) and several walking and cycling trails. There is a sculpture trail, two food chain puzzle trails and a "Who I am?" course for children. Loch Ard Forest is home to a varied

Loch Ard Forest

wildlife population including red and roe deer and the rare water vole. The car park has a lovely middle-of-the-forest feel with picnic tables and a forest sculpture; "Sol Stood Still" by Rob Mulholland.

The B829 Beyond Aberfoyle

Loch Ard is in three parts, joined by narrow bands of water. From here the River Forth begins its journey to the sea. On a small island off the far shore (GR 473014) are the ruins of 15th century Murdoch's Castle. Murdoch was Scottish Regent when James 1 was released from imprisonment in England. Murdoch was executed and his lands forfeited.

The road continues winding its way along the loch beneath Ben Venue. In summer crossbills can sometimes be spotted amongst the conifer trees, their favoured habitat, and ospreys enjoy fishing on the loch.

Kinlochard

Kinlochard, at the head of the loch, is Forestry Commission managed. Here, Rob Roy accosted the bailiff and took his money. Much of the 1953 Rob Roy film was shot locally.

It is a popular starting point for the ascent of Ben Venue (727m/2384') where golden eagles soar over the craggy peaks.

Great Times Scotland is based at Ledard Farm, a 17th century working hill farm. Behind is the waterfall featured in Scott's novels, "Rob Roy" and "Waverley." The farm was the first youth hostel in Britain. Today it is the place to learn about the Jacobites, handle their weapons, savour a dram, meet sheep dogs or try your hand at shooting clay pigeons or targets on the indoor rifle range. Pre booked visits only. www.greattimescotland.com.

Forest Hills is a luxurious hotel & self

Forest Hills

catering complex with a restaurant overlooking the loch.

Go Country, on the loch shore, offers a wide range of water activities as well as abseiling, archery, quad biking, canoe and bike hire and fishing permits. Tel: 01877 387750 www.gocountryleisure.co.uk

"Go Country"

The Wee Blether Tea Room is definitely

Wee Blether Tea Rooms

not one to drive past! Superb freshly cooked food, amazing home-made cakes and baguettes named after Scottish characters, a quirky garden (spot the carved squirrel!) complete with balcony overlooking the loch. Gluten free bread available. (Interesting

wallpaper in the loo!) Open daily Mothers' Day to end of Oct. 10.00am. – 5.00pm. **The Loch Ard Sailing Club**, (dinghies) is affiliated to the Royal Yachting Association.

Mill of Chon, at the western end of Loch Ard, was once a corn mill.

Couligarten has a car park and trails into the forest and around the southern shore, from where there is a good view of Eilean Gorm (Loch Ard's largest island), a crannog and the remains of Murdoch's Castle (see page 37). Exploring the island is popular with canoeists; there is a small bothy on Eilean Gorm. Near Couligarten is an impressive aqueduct, over 100 yards (90m) long and part of the Glasgow Water Scheme.

The Teapot, marked on the map, was once a "cottage inn" selling illicit whisky.

Loch Dhu & Loch Chon

Loch Chon

Beyond Kinlochard one of the most scenic parts of the route meanders amongst mature oaks, birch and ash. Bracken lines the road by Loch Dhu ("The Black Loch") which is joined to Loch Chon ("Loch of the Dog") by a short stretch of water. Burns tumble towards the loch under rustic little stone bridges and in summer the edges of Loch Chon fill with water lilies. However, the scene was not always so tranquil: The road was once lined with well spaced Nissan huts full of ammunition – a WWII store. A lay-by at the side of the loch affords a good view across to waterfalls tumbling down from Beinn Dubh. Beyond Loch Chon the terrain changes to open moorland between Loch Arklet to the west and Loch Katrine to the east, an area covered with heather from late July onwards. A junction is reached: Half a mile (0.8km) to the right is Stronachlachar on Loch Katrine; to the left the road runs four miles (6.5km) down to Inversnaid. (Either route requires a return to this junction.)

Loch Katrine (West) (see also the section on Loch Katrine east on page 45).

Owned by Scottish Water, Loch Katrine is 8 miles (13km) long. Much of its attraction is its remoteness. Although the Gaelic name "Cateran" denotes a Highland robber, a more charming explanation for the name tells of Katrine, a virgin who guarded a fountain of pure water. A goblin made the fountain overflow and form the loch in which she was drowned as revenge for his unrequited love.

There is no public roadway around the loch but the 22 miles (36km) of shoreline is accessible by track. Two miles (6km) east of Stronachlachar is Royal Cottage, built for Queen Victoria but unused by her. Nearby is the first of many aqueducts, built for the Glasgow Water Scheme. It became fashionable to visit Loch Katrine after 1810 when Sir Walter

The Loch Katrine Water Scheme

Glasgow's rapid 19th century growth created the need for a new supply of clean drinking water. Glasgow Corporation embarked upon one of the grandest engineering schemes of the time, led by Robert Stewart whose own fiancée had died of typhoid. The scheme was begun in 1856 and officially opened by Queen Victoria in October 1859. Designed by engineer J.F.Bateman (1810 – 1889), it involved damming Loch Katrine and piping water twenty six miles (42km) to Glasgow. The level of the loch was raised so water would use only gravity to carry it to Milngavie outside the city. Between 1885 and 1914 the scheme was enlarged and Loch Arklet included. Much of the material was ferried to Inversnaid by boat then hauled up to the site by aerial ropeway. Glasgow's Stewart Memorial Fountain in Kelvingrove Park commemorates the inspiration of Robert Stewart. The ornate fountain features themes from Scott's "The Lady of The Lake" and was restored to full working order in 2009 for the 150th anniversary of the Loch Katrine Water Scheme.

Scott published "The Lady of The Lake", a romantic poem about clan struggles involving a heroine called Ellen, set around Loch Katrine. Scott's poem took the world by storm, was translated into several languages and even made into operas. In 1825 Franz Schubert (1797-1829) set to music three Ellen songs from the poem, one which went on to become one of the most well known - "Ave Maria." Ellen's Isle is at the eastern end of the loch.

Stronachlachar Pier is the destination for the "Sir Walter Scott" which has been steaming up and down the loch for over 100 years, as well as other boats. (See section on Trossachs Pier on p45).

The Pier Tea Rooms, in the original Victorian building, are open daily from 10.00am during the holiday season. There are stunning views over the loch, real coffee, home-made soup and scones. The pier club sandwich is a good lunchtime filler! Boat hire, fishing permits, cycle hire available as well as daily newspapers! (sometimes hard to obtain in parts of the Highlands). Doggy water bowl for thirsty canine visitors.

Pier Tea Rooms, Stronachlachar

Factor's Island near the pier is where Rob Roy held the Duke of Montrose's factor hostage after his home and wife were attacked. **Glengyle** at the western end of the loch, is accessible by foot or cycle from the pier. Rob Roy was born here and there is an ancient MacGregor burial ground.

Loch Arklet to Inversnaid

Lock Arklet

The Inversnaid road follows the northern shore of Loch Arklet, a reservoir which feeds Loch Katrine via an aqueduct. **Corriearklet Farm,** where Rob Roy married Helen MacGregor Campbell, is half way down Loch Arklet. **Loch Arklet Dam**, at the western end of the loch, is impressive - 350 yards (320m) long and 35' (10.6m) high. A plaque commemorates those who inspired the

Loch Arklet Dam

project from 1909 to 1914. From below the dam a steep walk follows Arklet Water to Loch Lomond. **Inversnaid Bunk House and Top Bunk Bistro** is a converted church and one of

the most welcoming places in Scotland! As well as hostel and self catering accommodation, the Top Bunk Bistro dishes up imaginatively cooked food, including a full vegetarian menu. There are comfy seats, real ales, newspapers to read and original stained glass to admire.

The adjacent graveyard contains unmarked graves of late 19th century "navvies" (navigation labourers) who worked on the dams and aqueducts. Free internet & Wi-Fi. Open 12.00 noon – 4.00pm. 6.00pm. – 9.00pm. (seasonal) On the hill opposite the bunk house is a pile of stones, all that remains of the school attended by Rob Roy. **Rob Roy's View**: A hundred yards (90m)

beyond the bunkhouse is signposted a car park for Rob Roy's view. The bridge over the Arklet Burn, functional rather than aesthetic, was constructed in 1965 by The 129 Engineer Regiment of The Territorial Army.

Craigroyston Woods, accessed from the car park, is a historic native oak woodland - a popular habitat for pine marten.

In May 1940 this area was mistakenly bombed: During an anthrax outbreak huge pyres were built to burn the carcasses of infected animals. A German pilot mistook the glow for the lights of Glasgow and dropped over twenty bombs before realising his mistake.

Inversnaid

Inversnaid

The road twists steeply down the final descent to Loch Lomond, where there is a large car park, a hotel, a bird reserve and access to the West Highland Way. In 1715 Rob Roy and two hundred followers left here by boat on an infamous cattle raid. Sir Walter Scott, Wordsworth and Queen Victoria also visited Inversnaid. Information boards at the car park give an insight into the history and nature of the

place. Seen across the loch are huge pipes carrying water from Loch Sloy to Inveruglas power station. During summer, various boats call at the jetty.

The Inversnaid Hotel is owned by Lochs and Glens Holidays. It was originally built in 1820 as a hunting lodge for the Duke of Montrose but later became a hotel. During the second half of the 19th century it was a popular part of the "Trossachs Tour". Tourists arrived by steamer from Balloch. Horse drawn carriages conveyed them up the steep hill from the hotel and on to Loch Katrine. This was the last scheduled horse drawn coach service in Britain, running until 1937. Today, as well as organised tours, the hotel offers accommodation to other visitors. It has its own launch and small harbour for ferrying guests to and from Inveruglas on the western shore of the loch. The hotel is open for most of the year.

Inversnaid Waterfall: South of the hotel the final waterfall of the Arklet Burn cascades below a footbridge into a pool before entering Loch Lomond. The scene was immortalised by Gerard Manley Hopkins in a poem entitled simply "Inversnaid". In the 1939 version of "The 39 Steps" Hannay hides by the waterfall from a passing police boat.

Rob Roy's Cave, 1 mile (1.6km) north of the hotel, is a gap in the rock, rather than an actual cave. Earlier it was used by Robert The Bruce after The Battle of Dalrigh. (See page 21).

RSPB Reserve: The reserve covers nearly 1000 acres of shoreline, woodland and crag. At one time the woods here were coppiced to produce charcoal for iron smelting. Trees include oak, ash, birch, rowan and alder with its lovely miniature cones. The trees and  varied terrain provides habitats for many different birds including wood warblers, dippers, grouse and redstarts. In summer the woods have a carpet of bluebells, anemones and wild garlic. Red deer, roe deer and wild goats can be spotted more easily than the shy badgers who also live here. An information board shows what to look out for. Three trails criss-cross the reserve: The West Highland Way, a woodland nature trail and a track to a renovated sheep fank (enclosure).

RSPB Reserve,

Public Toilets
Aberfoyle – car park
Stronachlachar Pier
Internet Access
Aberfoyle Post Office

6.   THE TROSSACHS

The Trossachs is a small gorge between Ben A'an and Ben Venue, Loch Katrine and Loch Achray. However, the name is used to include the wider area between Loch Katrine, Aberfoyle and Callander. It is an area of rugged crags and tranquil lochs, home to red squirrels, otters, red and roe deer, peregrine falcons and golden eagles.

This has been a popular destination since the 19th century: William and Dorothy Wordsworth visited with Samuel Coleridge in 1803. Sir Walter Scott's stay near Loch Katrine inspired several works (see below and pages 45 and 47) causing tourists to flock to the area.

The route is scenic in either direction, here described clockwise from Aberfoyle where the A821 climbs steeply into Achray Forest.

Sir Walter Scott (1771 – 1832) Poet and author:
Born in 1771 to Walter Scott (senior) and Anne Rutherford of Edinburgh, young Walter wrote poetry from a very early age. His most notable work, "The Lady of The Lake", was inspired by a holiday taken in The Trossachs with his wife, Charlotte - "The Lake" in fact being Loch Katrine. The poem was published in 1810 and within some eight months had sold 25,000 copies. A musical play based on the poem had performances in London, Edinburgh and New York - one of the songs was "Hail to the Chief", now better known to announce the arrival of the President of the USA. A further work, his 1817 novel "Rob Roy", also has connections with The Trossachs. (See page 47.) Scott died in September 1832 at Abbotsford in The Borders. He is buried next to his wife in Dryburgh Abbey.
The steamer which now plies Loch Katrine bears his name and visitors to Edinburgh's Princes Street will recognise the tribute to Sir Walter Scott in the form of the "Scott Monument."

THE TROSSACHS

1 David Marshall Lodge
2 Go Ape
3 "Lumberjills" statue
4 Disused slate quarry
5 Viewpoint
6 Three Lochs Forest Drive
7 Loch Achray Hotel
8 Loch road (bicycles, walking)
9 Ellen's Isle
10 An Tigh Mor
11 The Trossachs Church
12 Little Drum car park
13 Venachar Lochside Boathouse
14 Dunmore Fort
15 Samson's Putting Stone
16 Gartchonzie Bridge
17 Invertrossachs Estate
18 Trossachs Tryst
19 Coilhallan Wood
20 Rednock Farm Trekking
21 Castle Rednock (private land)
22 Inchmahome Priory
23 Port of Menteith Church
24 The Lake Hotel
25 Lake of Menteith Fisheries

TROSSACHS PIER
Loch Cruises   Katrinewheelz
Glasgow Corporation Drinking Fountain
Nature play area Katrine Café
Katrine Gifts

BRIG o' TURK
The Byre Inn
Ruskin Trail
The Bicycle Tree
Tea Rooms
Brig o' Turk Graveyard
Glen Finglas Trails

P - car park

Callander
R. Teith
A873
B822
L. Rusky
A81
A84
Kilmahog
L. Lubnaig
A821
Glen Finglas
Brig o' Turk
L. Venachar
L. Achray
Dukes Pass
The Trossachs
Ben A'an
Ben Venue
Loch Katrine
Trossachs Pier
Port of Menteith
Lake of Menteith
B8034
Aberfoyle
B829
Inversnaid
A81

N

The Lady of The Lake: The Poem
Scott's epic poem tells of the feud between King James V of Scotland and Clan Douglas and the subsequent attempts of Malcolm Graeme, James Fitz-James (the King in disguise) and Roderick Dhu to woe Ellen Douglas while she is exiled on an island on Loch Katrine. Ellen intervenes and love wins through. The poem was translated into many languages, made into musicals and even an opera.

The David Marshall Lodge is a superb Forestry Commission facility, the start of several walking and cycling trails, one to the 16m (52') Little Fawn Falls. Attractions include a café with stunning views, an adventure playground and "Go Ape" – an exhilarating way to experience the forest at speed - via one of two 420m zip wires! Other facilities include CCTV of pine martens and an osprey eyrie, live cameras on squirrel and bird feeders, a gift shop, children's wildlife "spotter" sheets etc. A statue commemorates "lumberjills" – ladies of the WWII Land Army Women's Timber Corps.
Disused quarry (see pages 34 & 36) After the quarry closed, over fifty years ago, the buildings disappeared, except for the "Gaffer's" house. On a ridge above the quarry twelve cairns mark where locals died in a fight with cattle reivers (rustlers).
The Duke's Pass, built in 1885 by the Duke of Montrose, was originally a toll road. At the highest point a car park overlooks much of the Trossachs. A wheelchair friendly-track leads to another viewpoint.

The Three Lochs Forest Drive: Between Apr. and Oct. (10.00am – 5.00pm) vehicles can go "off road" on a 7.5 mile (12km) track past Lochan Reoidhte and Lochs Drunkie and Achray.
The Loch Achray Hotel nestles at the bottom of Duke's Pass against the majestic backdrop of Ben Venue rising to over 727m (2385'). The hotel, built in 1870 as a hunting lodge, now mostly welcomes guests of Lochs and Glens Holidays. (Bar open to non residents).

The Trossachs Pier & Loch Katrine (East)
(See also the section on Loch Katrine on page 39.)
A short road branches off to The Trossachs Pier at the eastern end of Loch Katrine, from where the Sir Walter Scott (see page 46) and other vessels depart. The SS Sir Walter Scott was not the loch's first pleasure boat: A galley, "Water Witch", rowed by locals carried visitors to Jonathan's Island to sample whisky from an illicit still! In 1843 a paddle steamer, PS Gypsy, appeared but was scuttled

SS Sir Walter Scott at The Trossachs Pier

The SS Sir Walter Scott

For over a hundred years Loch Katrine has been home to this wonderful steam boat, the last remaining one of its kind still in service in Scotland. It was built in 1899 by William Denny & Sons Ltd. of Dumbarton, dismantled, its parts carefully numbered and then carried on barges up the River Leven to Inversnaid on Loch Lomond. It was then transported by horse and cart to Stronachlachar on Loch Katrine to be reassembled.

The boat is over 33m (110') long, nearly 6m (19') wide and weighs 110 tons. For her centenary in 1999 she underwent an extensive refurbishment. Her original engines, now powered by smokeless bio fuel, still propel her almost silently up and down the loch daily between April and October. The embarkation point is reached along a long covered walkway with interesting displays and tableaux.

(deliberately sunk) by the disgruntled Water Witch crew. A replacement paddle steamer "Rob Roy" arrived, on which Queen Victoria sailed when she came to open the water works in 1859. It remained in use until 1900. The car park has an ornate drinking fountain, provided by Glasgow Corporation in April 1955 to commemorate the Centenary of the water works scheme (see inset on p40).

The Katrine Café (licensed) serves light snacks including freshly baked scones, home-made cakes, jacket potatoes and salads.

Katrine Gifts, in the former boathouse, sells souvenirs and books.

The Katrine Ice Cream Kiosk sells ices, hot and cold drinks, sandwiches and snacks.

"Lady of The Lake" is a relaxing way to cruise the loch, in the saloon or on the top deck - trips to Stronachlachar or shorter trips among the islands. Booking: Tel: 01877 332000

Katrinewheelz – hire bicycles, tandems, children's tag-alongs, electric bikes and buggies, even take a bike by boat to Stronachlachar and cycle back. Booking advisable 24 hours in advance. Tel: 01877 376366 cycling@lochkatrine.com

Katrinewheelz

Around the shore: The public road ends at the pier but walkers and cyclists may enjoy the beautiful twelve mile (19km) private road along the north shore and round the head of the loch to Stronachlachar. (see page 39) Information boards impart fascinating information, including the fact that from the musical of "The Lady of The Lake" came the tune "Hail to the Chief" – now better known heralding the arrival of The President of the USA. (See page 43.) Watch out for

> **Rob Roy: The Novel**
> This is the story of a merchant's son who, in his efforts to avenge a wrong done to his father, travels to the Highlands where he is helped by Rob Roy, the famous, real-life outlaw. Another earlier novel about Rob Roy was Daniel Defoe's "Highland Rogue".

otters, red squirrels, deer, pine marten and the occasional red kite or osprey.

Ellen's Isle ("Eilean Molach"), about a mile (1.5 km) from the pier, was once used as a refuge for MacGregor women.

Brenachoile Pier featured in the 2008 version of the film "The Thirty Nine Steps."

Portnellan is the site of a MacGregor burial ground, on an artificial island built by Glasgow Corporation when both shoreline and burial ground were raised. The lintel over the entrance bears the MacGregor crest and motto "E'en da bait spair nacht." ("Even do but spare not.")

Glengyle, at the foot of the glen of the same name, was the birthplace of the infamous Rob Roy MacGregor in 1671. Another burial ground can be seen near Glengyle House.

Loch Achray

This is a beautiful loch, fringed with oak trees and heather and renowned for its reflections of Ben A'an, Ben Venue and the Achray forest. Car parks at the western end provide access to Ben Venue (727m/ 2385') and Ben A'an, ("The Pinnacle") which is a small conical peak. For the less energetic, the car park has super-tame chaffinches hopping about and excellent maps giving a 3D overview of the area.

An Tigh Mor is a grand turreted building dating from 1849 to accommodate the influx of tourists. Now a time share resort, a nearby milepost gives the distance as ¼

Loch Achray & Ben Venue

mile (0.4km) to "The Trossachs Hotel". As elsewhere, the ornate mileposts were placed for Queen Victoria's visit. Film enthusiasts may recognise the hotel as St Catherine's School in "The Thirty Nine Steps".

The Trossachs Church looks out over Loch Achray, its gate guarded by a gnarled oak tree. The church was built in 1849 and has latticed windows and roof tiles forming an unusual diagonal pattern. The graveyard has some old crosses and

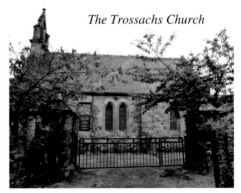

The Trossachs Church

interesting gravestones. One for a Henderson Dunmore also bears a poignant inscription to Hugh P. Thomson of the Cameron Highlanders who "...*gave his life to shield his master*". Church services: First Sunday of the month.

The Byre Inn, quarter of a mile (0.4km) west of Brig o' Turk, is a quirky pub and restaurant in a converted byre serving real ales, wine and an imaginative menu. (Try the home-made parsnip and apple

The Byre Inn

soup). The outside eating area has old tractor seats around upturned barrels. Open most of the year.

Brig o' Turk

The present 19th century stone bridge replaced a 17th century wooden structure, the original village having probably developed at a ford over Finglas Water. The name derives partly from "tuirc" - a wild boar, once hunted locally. The village found itself on the tourist route after Queen Victoria's visit. Legend reports that the Queen asked to meet twenty-four stone landlady Kate Ferguson, known as "Muckle Kate" because of her size. ("Muckle" - a dialect word for "large.") The Queen gave her a gold sovereign. Other visitors included William and Dorothy Wordsworth and poet Samuel Coleridge.

During the mid 1800s the village became a popular summer residence for artists. These included John Ruskin, the leading art critic of the time, his protégé John Everett Millais and, later, the Glasgow Boys – a group of artists whose work revolutionised Scottish art between 1880 – 1900.

Behind the village hall is a large car park. The public road ends less than a mile (1.6km) from the main road but makes an interesting detour.

The Tea Room is quaint. Open all day.

The Bicycle Tree is one of Scotland's quirkier sights – an ancient sycamore tree which has grown around a bicycle, the handlebars still visible. The tree is behind a tin hut opposite where the "smiddy" used to stand. The blacksmith was in the habit of hanging things on the branches and forgetting about them. One story claims the bicycle was left there affectionately by villagers following his death - at eighty two years old after forty eight years as village blacksmith. Another story cites a villager who hung the bike there before he went off to The Great War – and never returned.

The Bicycle Tree

The Ruskin Trail: Beyond The Bicycle Tree, an opening in the wall leads to the Ruskin Trail to where Millais painted his famous portrait of Ruskin in 1853.

Brig o' Turk Graveyard has some fascinating gravestones, including an elaborate coffin shaped memorial bearing a shepherd's crook.

Glen Finglas is predominantly ancient woodland. For over four hundred years it was a royal hunting forest, playground to the Stewart Kings. The glen was dammed in 1965 to form a three hundred acre reservoir to feed Loch Katrine. The Woodland Trust bought the estate in 1996. The glens running down to the reservoir are popular with walkers. There is a small car park at the end of the public road or the main Glen Finglas car park half a mile east (0.8km) of the village.

Glen Finglas Trails: Half a mile (0.8km) east of Brig o' Turk is the Forestry Commission car park. An interactive

Interactive display

display enables visitors to listen to 18th century King's Foresters and modern day workers. There are laminated children's sheets for a "feely box trail". Walking and cycling trails including a strenuous thirteen mile (21km) circuit to follow the reservoir before climbing up Glen Meann and circling Meall Cala ("The Mell"). A

less strenuous walk climbs Lendrick Hill to the Royal Mail Grove of Trees with views over Loch Venachar and the Achray Forest.

The Little Drum Car Park, a mile (1.6km) east of Brig o' Turk, is the start of several walks, including Little Drum Woods or across Brig o' Turk Mires, a wetland Area of Special Scientific Interest, once the village curling pond.

Loch Venachar: The North Shore

The loch is nearly four miles (5.7 km) long, half a mile (0.8km) wide and 33m (111') at its deepest. It enters the Eas Gobhain, via a dam with eleven sluices and two salmon ladders. It then becomes the River Teith which eventually joins with River Forth. The dam was built in 1859, the same time as that on Loch Katrine. Water from Loch Venachar is used to maintain river levels. One definition of "Venachar" is "a fair valley". Another suggests "bheannchair" – horn shaped, as was Loch Venachar before the dam was built. Queen Victoria found this loch so picturesque in 1859 that she allowed herself to be rowed across to the other side.

The loch contains trout, salmon, pike and perch for shore or boat angling. Permits are available from various places including James Bayne in Callander (www.jamesbayne.co.uk). The sluices controlling the flow of water into the Teith are situated at the eastern end of the loch, where FitzJames and Roderick Dhu had their epic fight in Sir Walter Scott's "The Lady of The Lake". The Rob Roy Way joins Loch Venachar at its eastern end. From here there are views of Ben

Gullipen, Beinnn Dearg and Ben Venue to the west.

The trees around the shore make this a hospitable place for pretty black and white goldeneye ducks who nest in small holes in trees. They can be seen throughout the year. In winter overseas visitors from Iceland and Northern Europe arrive, amongst them whooper swans - recognisable by the flash of gold on their beaks.

Venachar Lochside: This modern building is a café during the day and a licensed restaurant

at night. Enjoy home baked snacks, lunch or dinner and the chance to take home a piece of the scenery from the paintings for sale.
Open all year, daily from 9.00am. (10.00am. in winter) – 9.30pm.
The Bird of Prey Viewing Trail begins next to the restaurant.
Venachar Lochside Boathouse offers boat trips on the loch as well as motor boat and fishing equipment hire, permits etc. Tel: 01877 330011

From the eastern end of Loch Venachar the A821 joins the A84 at Kilmahog but a minor road crosses the river and doubles back along the southern shore of Loch Venachar towards Invertrossachs House.
Bochastle Hill: From the minor road/A821 junction is a short but bracing walk up Bochastle Hill to Dunmore Fort - the remains of an Iron Age fort. An information board shows how the fort would have looked. Further around the hill

Samson's Putting Stone

is Samson's Stone, the legendary putting stone of a local giant, a "glacial erratic" – a 3m (10') boulder carried from Glen Dochart by a glacier.

Loch Venachar to Callander - A821 Bochastle and Kilmahog see page 59.

Loch Venachar to Callander – minor road
Gartchonzie Bridge: The minor road leaves the A821 to cross the Eas Gobhain via a beautiful two arched stone structure dating from 1777, built on the former estate of the Duke of Perth when it was forfeited after the 1745 Jacobite Uprising.
South Loch Venachar & The Invertrossachs Estate: The south shore is accessible on foot, bicycle or horse along the private Invertrossachs road from the eastern end of the loch, a favourite with heron and goldeneye. The estate is privately owned but welcomes responsible visitors and provides a car park at the end of the public road.
Trossachs Tryst: Owned by the same people as Katrinewheelz (see page 46), this spacious, modern hostel has a self catering kitchen, dormitories and family rooms and also offers guided cycling

trips, repairs and cycles, spares and clothing for sale. www.trossachstryst  **Coilhallan Wood** is Forestry Commission managed woodland with a multi use path linking with other trails in the area. Entrance/car park at Gartchonzie.

Callander to Aberfoyle

From Callander the A81 road crosses the "Lots of Callander", an area divided into "lots" after being forfeited by the Duke of Perth after the 1745 Jacobite Rebellion. The road climbs to pretty Loch Rusky then descends again with good views of the Lake of Menteith, with Inchmahome at its centre.

Castle Rednock Farm Trekking Centre: This working hill farm, owned by the same family for over a century, now operates a pony trekking and outdoor centre offering Nordik trekking, segway trekking, orienteering, Shetland pony driving and a family nature trail. www.rednock.horseriders.co.uk

Castle Rednock: To the west of the A81 (GR: 600023) are the remains of Castle Rednock, possibly built between 1250 and 1310 by The Sheriff of Dumbarton, James (John) Menteith, otherwise known as Fause John: "Fause" is a Scottish word for "false" - it was he who betrayed William Wallace to Government troops. The castle is thought to have been rebuilt in 1580 by George Graham of Rednock. The present Rednock Farm was built in 1800 largely from stone taken from the castle.

The Lake of Menteith & Inchmahome Priory

Set against a backdrop of the Menteith Hills, this is Scotland's only "lake" – a fact attributed to either Sir Walter Scott, said to have renamed it, or a Dutch cartographer reputed to have misread "loch" or "laigh" (low lying land) for "lake". It is one of Scotland's most atmospheric stretches of water, largely because of Inchmahome at its centre (Gaelic "Innis Mo Cholmaig" - "Island of Saint Colmaig"). The Augustinian Monastery was founded in 1238 by the Earl of Menteith. Robert Bontine Cunningham Graham (see page 33) is buried on the island.

The island and ruins are managed by Historic Scotland who run a small ferry during summer. The ferry staff are

Inchmahome

extremely informative. To "call" the ferry a mounted disc is turned round to attract attention. Information boards give a fascinating glimpse of the daily lives of the monks. The carvings and effigies in the chapter house are remarkable. Visitors to the island included Robert The Bruce three times between 1306 and 1310. In 1547 Inchmahome became the island refuge of the infant Mary Queen of Scots. Two other islands are the Isle of Dogs and Inch Talla, the latter having the ruins of a 15th century castle.

The lake is a designated Site of Special Scientific Interest because of its flora and fauna: Otters play at the edge of the lake, which in summer is fringed with at least three different types of water lilies. On the damp wooded shores many fungi thrive and the lake is a bird watchers' paradise: Goldeneye, tufted ducks and herons can be seen throughout the year. Willow warblers appear between April and September while the colder weather brings great numbers of geese and whooper swans. The area is an important roosting area for pink footed and greylag geese. At dawn and dusk large numbers fly in and out of the area but perhaps an even more impressive sight is great crested grebes performing their courting rituals – "standing" upright on the water facing each other and flapping their wings.

The Lake of Menteith has two further reasons for fame: Much of A.J Cronin's "Dr. Finlay's Casebook" was filmed here. Also, the lake has long been a venue for the sport of curling, in the past occasionally the scene of a "bonspiel" – a tournament held on a frozen lake. Strict rules govern how thick the ice must be: In recent years health and safety issues have prevailed.

Port of Menteith Church
Designed by John Honeyman and built in 1878 on the site of an earlier church, this pretty gothic style building is renowned for its trefoil window by Stephen Adam. In the graveyard is a mausoleum of the Grahams of Gartmore.

Lake of Menteith Fisheries: Boat hire and permits for fly fishing on the lake for pike and trout. Tel: 01877 385664

The Lake Hotel is tranquil with picture windows overlooking the loch, waterfront decking and decor chosen to reflect the setting. Originally a 19th century manse,

The Lake Hotel

the hotel offers formal and informal dining and has won several awards for the food it serves. Open all year.

Toilets
The Trossachs Pier
David Marshall Lodge
Aberfoyle – main car park
Inchmahome

Fishing on The Lake of Menteith

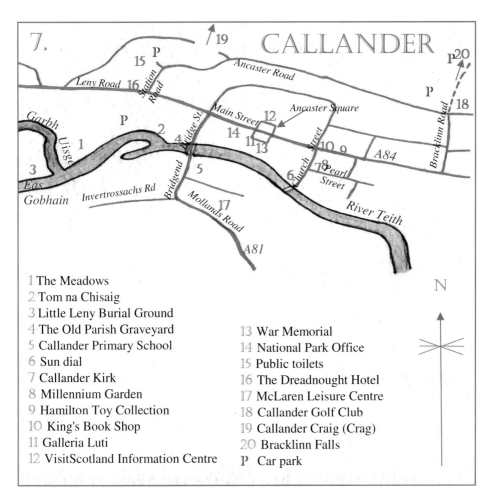

1 The Meadows
2 Tom na Chisaig
3 Little Leny Burial Ground
4 The Old Parish Graveyard
5 Callander Primary School
6 Sun dial
7 Callander Kirk
8 Millennium Garden
9 Hamilton Toy Collection
10 King's Book Shop
11 Galleria Luti
12 VisitScotland Information Centre

13 War Memorial
14 National Park Office
15 Public toilets
16 The Dreadnought Hotel
17 McLaren Leisure Centre
18 Callander Golf Club
19 Callander Craig (Crag)
20 Bracklinn Falls
P Car park

Callander lies close to the Highland Boundary Fault, literally where The Highlands meet The Lowlands. It is also the eastern gateway to The Trossachs. The wide main street is lined with elegant buildings, many shops and a large choice of accommodation and restaurants. Everywhere is evidence of Callander's past, stretching back to Neolithic times and, later, the Druids: To the west is 879m (2883') high Ben Ledi, "Hill of God", an ancient religious site.

The remains of a Roman fort are still visible west of Callander. Later, in the 6th century, St. Kessog arrived from Ireland. After the Jacobite defeat at Culloden the Government confiscated many estates and constructed a military road network with towns along the route. Callander was one such town.

In 1858 the railway arrived and Callander became part of a popular tour by rail, road and steamer from Glasgow and Stirling to Loch Lomond and The Trossachs. During the 1960s the streets of Callander became recognised nationally as Tannochbrae in the TV series "Dr. Finlay's Casebook."

The "Story in The Stones": Pavement markers, information boards and a leaflet available from the VisitScotland Information Centre provide an excellent heritage trail around the town.

The Meadows is a pleasant riverside area combining a car park, playground and picnic area.

Tom na Chisaig is a conical mound, probably a former "motte" – surrounded

Tom na Chisaig

by a ditch and topped with a fortified structure. Although named after St. Kessog, it was constructed centuries later. The mound overlooks the old parish graveyard, site of the old kirk until a new one was built in Ancaster Square in 1773. During the 19th century Tom na Chisaig was used as an outdoor place of worship prior to the building of Callander Kirk in South Church Street.

Roman Fort: From The Meadows a walk upstream leads to the confluence of the Eas Gobhain and Garbh Uisge then along the disused railway to the site of the fort, visible as a series of earthworks.

Little Leny Burial Ground is just south of the cycle track on the old railway. It is a Clan Buchanan burial ground. Dugald Buchanan, the famous Gaelic poet, lies here.

Bridge Street and the south bank of the river

Bridge Street

The 1908 arched bridge carrying the A81 over the river is a Grade B listed structure. Its red sandstone facing belies its concrete construction. It replaced an earlier 1764 bridge, before which a ferry crossed the Teith at this point. At one end of the bridge two lovely, old cast iron lamps remain.

The Old Parish Graveyard:

Old Parish Graveyard

The hexagonal watch tower deterred body-snatchers from removing corpses to sell for medical research.

Callander Primary School is a beautiful colonnaded building. It was originally The McLaren High School, founded and paid for by local benefactor Donald McLaren (1786 – 1854). A path leads down the side of the school to a footbridge over the river.

South Church Street

Sun Dial: By the footbridge in South Church Street is a beautiful limestone sundial, donated to the town by Lord Esher after WWI and recently restored by Historic Scotland. A modern graph provides time corrections for different months of the year.

Sun dial

Callander Kirk (1844) was formerly St. Bride's Church but amalgamated in 1985 with St Kessog's Church from Ancaster Square. It has a gallery illustrating the history of the Kirk. Of note are the beautiful stained glass windows to honour local men who died in WW1 and a carved chair - gift from Norwegian soldiers stationed at Callander in WWII.

Callander Kirk Millennium Garden is a peaceful oasis with two wrought iron memorial seats, one featuring a ball of wool, needles, bobbin

St. Kessog's Bell

and the SWRI logo (Scottish Women's Rural Institute). The other has flowers, crosses and hearts. Nearby is St. Kessog's Bell, used in St. Kessog's Church from 1784 until 1985.

Main Street - East of Ancaster Square

The wide pavements and 19th century, red sandstone buildings make Main Street a pleasant place to stroll. Scotland's oldest bakery was founded in Callander in 1830 by Donald Campbell. Six generations later, the Campbells are still producing delicious shortbread, available from Woollen Mill outlets. It is not possible to mention all the wonderful establishments in Callander. What follows is a selection, leaving readers to experience the joy of discovery!

The Roman Camp Hotel, one of Callander's hidden gems, takes its name from the earthworks visible from the hotel, at one time thought to be Roman. The hotel was originally one of The Duke of Perth's hunting lodges. In 1897 it was bought by Lord Esher. The house was later sold and became a hotel. One of Lady Esher's tapestries still hangs in the hotel.

The Hamilton Toy Collection is one of

Hamilton Toy Collection

the most comprehensive collections of children's toys, books and games in the UK, for the sheer quantity of exhibits and the range of different collections under one roof. Open Apr. – Oct. and some half terms.

Munchies Coffee Shop and licensed restaurant is a delightful, traditional restaurant with fresh flowers and pen and ink drawings of old Callander. It serves all day breakfasts, old fashioned high teas and irresistible home-made desserts.

Munchies

The Crags Hotel is a friendly place, its restaurant serving simple but well cooked food (summer months only). There is a cosy public bar and a room with a four poster.

King's Bookshop sell second-hand books, has an antique table at which to sit and read from a choice of books including beautifully restored volumes bound on the premises.

The Waverley Hotel: Claymores and targes, award-winning cask ales, a beer garden, live music during the summer and sports TV all make this a lively place. Food served daily from 12.00 noon – 9.00pm.

Macmillan Wine is an independent merchant with a huge selection of wines and unusual whiskies, including 40 year old malts.

Ancaster Square

Ancaster Square, named after the Duke of Perth's successor, The Earl of Ancaster, is a pleasant place to sit and watch the World go by.

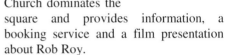

Ancaster Square

VisitScotland in the former St. Kessog's Church dominates the square and provides information, a booking service and a film presentation about Rob Roy.

Deli Ecosse Café, tucked away in a quiet corner of the square, offers a relaxed atmosphere, an interesting menu of Scottish sourced food and home baking accompanied by tea, coffee or a glass of wine.

Pip's Coffee House, with pavement seating, is a pleasant place to enjoy a coffee.

The War Memorial in the square is topped with a majestic, crowned lion rampant.

D. Campbell and Son: An award winning butcher's whose pies, haggis, black and white puddings and burgers are made on the premises.

Galleria Luti is a stylish, family run gallery specialising in original contemporary Scottish art including that of Peter Luti, husband and father to the co-owners of the gallery, themselves talented artists, one a jeweller.

Galleria Luti

Main Street West of Ancaster Square

Amy Johnson's World Famous Scottish Tablet has been made to the same recipe since 1926. ("Tablet" is not fudge: It is a lovely sugary confection, a national favourite with a texture all of its own.)

Loch Lomond & The Trossachs National Park Office: Have your UK National Parks visitor passport stamped, pick up some excellent information leaflets full of things to do and see and access their website. Open weekdays.

Callander Meadows Restaurant is a reasonably priced restaurant and coffee shop, also serving lighter lunches. Outside eating overlooking the river.

Mhor Bread produce a tempting array of modern and traditional breads including black buns and buttered bannocks. Next to the bread shop is a tea room.

The Crown Hotel has a reputation for good value, home cooked food, a warm welcome, live entertainment and has been a finalist in the Sunday Mail Pub of The Year Award. Live football on big screen TV.

The Whisky Shop sells a huge range of malt and blended whiskies. Knowledgeable staff and attractive displays make for an interesting experience.

The Old Bank is a family run tea room and restaurant in a former Royal Bank of Scotland branch, serving freshly prepared home-made food (including vegetarian and gluten free options), excellent coffee and renowned for its home made steak pie and stunning desserts. (Try the almond apricot meringue!)

Station Road has a large car park with public toilets, a launderette and an extremely helpful Post Office.

The Dreadnought Hotel, originally built in the 17th century, owes its name not to a warship but to the motto of Clan McNab. The chief built the hotel to accommodate clansmen. Steeped in history, the present building dates from the early 19th century and features beautiful wood panelling, stained glass windows and a carved head high on the building- reputedly that of a McNeish taken by the McNabs in a feud!

The Riverside Inn: A family-friendly place serving morning coffee, lunches, high teas etc.

The Old Rectory, combining a guest house, Gray's Restaurant and a "whisky library" containing over one hundred and fifty whiskies, is popular with visitors and locals alike - especially for its weekly live traditional music evenings.

Poppies Hotel & Restaurant is an independent, owner run hotel with a reputation for a friendly welcome, attention to detail, good food, a huge selection of malts and attentive but not fussy service.

Away from the town centre....

McLaren Leisure Centre: Mollands Road – swimming pool, indoor climbing wall, sauna.

Callander Golf Club: From its elevated position at the eastern end of the town the 18 hole course enjoys splendid views. Visitors welcome. The club is open for bar snacks and meals.

Callander Craig (Crags): From the car park, reached from Bracklinn Road, a path climbs through mixed woodland and beautiful rowan trees to the summit. At the highest point is The Queen

Victoria Diamond Jubilee Cairn, rebuilt in 1997 after the original collapsed.

The Bracklinn Falls: Keltie Water rushes down a narrow gorge above Callander to form these 15m (50') high falls. There is a

Bracklinn Falls

small car park at the start of the three quarters of a mile (1.2km) path, which passes beneath lovely old beech trees. The way eventually descends some steps to the falls. The brown, peat tinged water, flecked with twigs gives a hint to the name of the falls – "breac" being Gaelic for "speckled" and "linn" meaning a pool, a spot visited by Queen Victoria on one of her Scottish holidays. The bridge over the falls is modern, built after the 2004 floods washed away the iron footbridge. On the rocks above the falls stag beetles can sometimes be seen basking on the rocks,

looking quite plain and black until the sun catches their legs and underside and transforms them into beautiful fluorescent blue. South east of the falls are the remains

Stag Beetle

of an Iron Age fort and, at Auchenlaich Farm, Scotland's longest chambered cairn.

Callander Holiday Park: A thirty five acre, river-side park with lodges and static caravans set amongst mature woodland. Catch your own salmon or trout on the park's private beat on the Eas Gobhain river. Open mid Mar. – Oct.

Gart Caravan Park is a peaceful site which welcomes touring caravans and motor homes to a lovely parkland setting. Open Apr. – Mid Oct.

Keltie Bridge Caravan and Camping Park is a quiet riverside park for camping, caravans and motor homes, just off the A84. Open Apr. – Oct.

Public Toilets
Station Road car park
VisitScotland Information Centre,
Wi-Fi Access
VisitScotland Information Centre,

8. CALLANDER TO LOCHEARNHEAD & ST. FILLANS

Breadalbane ("Bràghaid Albainn" is the northern part of the Loch Lomond and The Trossachs National Park. Craggy peaks, high mountain pastures and deep glens provide habitats for a wide range of wildlife and plants, including alpine flowers and orchids. Breadalbane is steeped in the history of ancient tribes and clans: In the middle ages there was much clan rivalry, the Campbells having gained control by the 1700s. Breadalbane was a vast lawless area ruled by lairds. Subsistence was hard and fugitives from justice were common, two of the most famous being Robert The Bruce in the late 13th and early 14th centuries and Rob Roy MacGregor in the 17th and 18th (See page 62).

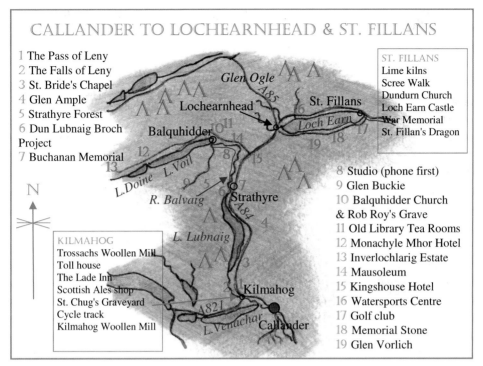

1 The Pass of Leny
2 The Falls of Leny
3 St. Bride's Chapel
4 Glen Ample
5 Strathyre Forest
6 Dun Lubnaig Broch Project
7 Buchanan Memorial

ST. FILLANS
Lime kilns
Scree Walk
Dundurn Church
Loch Earn Castle
War Memorial
St. Fillan's Dragon

8 Studio (phone first)
9 Glen Buckie
10 Balquhidder Church & Rob Roy's Grave
11 Old Library Tea Rooms
12 Monachyle Mhor Hotel
13 Inverlochlarig Estate
14 Mausoleum
15 Kingshouse Hotel
16 Watersports Centre
17 Golf club
18 Memorial Stone
19 Glen Vorlich

KILMAHOG
Trossachs Woollen Mill
Toll house
The Lade Inn
Scottish Ales shop
St. Chug's Graveyard
Cycle track
Kilmahog Woollen Mill

Kilmahog

Chug (Hog) was an early saint. Kilmahog (Gaelic: Cill mo Chùg) means cell of Hog, a cell being an outpost of a larger establishment. Kilmahog was important, guarding the Pass of Leny. There are remains of Roman ramparts in nearby fields and Leny House was home to Clan Buchanan's chief.

The Trossachs Woollen Mill houses a weaving exhibition, including a Hattersley loom. There is also a coffee shop and retail outlet for Scottish foods and knitwear and bags of chopped turnip for Hamish, the Highland bull who has become a tourist attraction in his own right.

Hamish

Toll House: By the junction of the A84 and A821 stands an early 19th century toll house.

Toll House, Kilmahog

Kilmahog Bridge, carrying the A821 away from the A84 over the Garbh Uisge, was built in 1777 as part of the new road network ordered by the Commissioners of Forfeited Estates after the Jacobite Uprising.

The Lade Inn is a must for Scottish Ale

enthusiasts! A small shop sells nearly a hundred and fifty Scottish beers, including

Scottish Real Ales Shop

the pub's specially brewed "Ladeout," "Waylade" and "Ladeback" ales. Open daily for lunch, bar snacks (until 5.00pm) and an evening restaurant menu.

St. Chug's Graveyard: Next to the Lade Inn are the remains of an ancient chapel and burial ground with gravestones from the 17th century and a "watch-house". Over the entrance hangs a bell thought to have been brought from the Lake of Menteith where it was used to summon the ferryman.

St. Chug's Graveyard

Bochastle: A short distance along the A821 is a car park. The disused railway is now a walking and cycling track and a popular starting point for climbing Ben Ledi.

Bochastle Roman Fort, visible as a series of earthworks, is also accessible from the track.

Kilmahog Woollen Mill, over two hundred and fifty years old, is one of Kilmahog's two original mills, its water wheel still intact. It is now a retail outlet

with a clan tartan centre, ancestry tracing service, whisky shop and a good selection of Harris Tweed and knitwear.

The Pass of Leny

From Kilmahog the road follows the Garbh Uisge ("rough water") also known as the River Leny, through the narrow oak and ash lined Pass of Leny. To the north west Ben Ledi rises to 879m (2875'). The disused railway follows the pass, now a scenic route for walkers and cyclists. This natural gateway to The Highlands has been strategically important throughout the ages, featuring in Sir Walter Scott's "A Legend of Montrose" and "The Lady of The Lake".

The Falls of Leny: A mile (1.6km) north of Kilmahog the falls are signposted from a roadside car park.

Loch Lubnaig: The river widens to become picturesque Loch Lubnaig. Its name possibly means "bent loch". It is fed from the north by the River Balvaig, both river and loch being popular with canoeists. Car parks provide access for boat launching. (Limited horsepower allowed.) Brown trout and salmon fishing permits available from James Bayne in Callander. A track opposite the more northerly of the two car parks leads to the remains of St. Bride's Chapel with ancient grave slabs.

The Rob Roy Way follows the western shore, while the A84 follows the eastern side and the old military road. From a lay-by at Ardchullarie More (GR 584136) a footpath climbs into Glen Ample. A small plaque on the signpost remembers R.T.Hooke, a member of the Scottish Rights of Way Society.

Immervoulin Caravan & Camping Park is family run, dog friendly and enjoys a riverside setting with good facilities and a well stocked shop. Open Mar. – Oct.

Strathyre

"Strathyre in its green nest among the hills is a pretty village with an inviting hostelry." (The Glory of Scotland by J.J. Bell 1932.) The village sits on the River Balvaig, a mile (1.6km) north of Loch Lubnaig. St. Cuthbert and St. Columba passed this way, as later did many cattle drovers. Crofting families settled here after being "cleared" from Balquhidder Glen by landowners. When the railway came in 1880, Strathyre had a station. In a garden on the main street is an attractive fountain featuring a heron – once the prize for the best kept station on the line.

At the southern end of the village a car park and picnic site adjoin the old railway, now a cycle and footpath leading to several routes through the Strathyre Forest. A narrow Forestry Commission track from the main road takes you alongside the Tigh an Eas Burn to Coille MacCaskill, a small wood mainly of pine and larch, dedicated to the memory of Don MacCaskill, forester, naturalist and well-known photographer. Three ancient stones mark the spot and an information board locates the start of the track through this delightful wood which joins two forestry roads and gives the walker further choices.

The Village Shop and Post Office sells fresh milk, bread, newspapers, sandwiches, postcards, kindling wood, wines and spirits etc.

The Buchanan Memorial: Strathyre was the birthplace of Dugald Buchanan (1716

– 1776), a religious poet, thought to have assisted the Killin minister James Stewart translate the New Testament into Gaelic. The memorial to him was erected in 1883.

Buchanan Memorial

The Dun Lubnaig Broch Project in the car park is a reconstruction of the building of an iron age broch, a fortified structure peculiar to Scotland.

Dun Lubnaig Broch Project

Creagan House: For a special dining experience, the polished refectory tables in the baronial dining hall sets the scene for an award winning menu best described as "classical French with Scottish overtones". Local produce, including home produced eggs and vegetables, is cooked with flair by the chef/proprietor. (Try the "Smokie in a pokie!") Open Mar – Jan (closed Wed & Thur.) Booking recommended. Tel: 01877 384638

The Ben Sheann Hotel: Built as a private house, it became the Star Inn in 1829 and later The Station Hotel. Food served all day. Dog friendly public bar. Open Easter – Oct.

The Inn at Strathyre: Open all year, serving food daily from 12.30pm. – 9.30pm, this is a popular place to eat and/ or stay. Real ale enthusiasts can enjoy a pint on the beer terrace, protected from the wildlife by one of those wonderful midge machines! Dogs welcome.

The Strathyre Forest: A small stone bridge beyond the village shop carries walkers, cyclists and careful motorists into the heart of the forest. Tumbling streams and mixed woodland make this a delightful detour. The minor road follows the River Balvaig. Before reaching Balquhidder a curious roadside collection of wooden carvings mark the studio which houses the work of painter Veronika Verden-Anderson and sculptor Edward Chadfield. Veronika is renowned for vibrant, primitive style paintings. Her partnership with Edward is unique: He

A Unique Partnership..

sculpts, she paints: The results are stunning. (Visitors please telephone first: 01877 384715.)

Glen Buckie, once part of a Royal forest, is a popular place from which to climb Creag Mhor.

Balquhidder

Signposted from the A84, Balquhidder is rich in history and is the final resting place of the infamous Rob Roy. Glen Balquhidder lies in the shadow of a ridge of hills known as The Braes of Balquhidder - the heart of "Rob Roy Country", seeing many violent inter-clan skirmishes as well as clashes with redcoats sent to quell Highland unrest. Centuries earlier, Robert The Bruce had also taken refuge in these hills. Car parking at the Village Hall.

Stronvar House was bought by David Carnegie in 1849. Once a fortified house dating from the 16th century most of the present house was built in Victorian times and added to considerably in the baronial style by architect David Bryce for David Carnegie. The house is now owned privately.

Balquhidder Church is Victorian.

Rob Roy MacGregor (1671 – 1734) – Folk hero

The subject of proven history, legend and novels, Rob Roy was born in February 1671 at Glengyle at the western end of Loch Katrine. In 1693 he married a cousin, Helen MacGregor.

His life could be called eventful in every sense of the word although much of what befell him was every bit "of the time". An active supporter and participant in the Jacobite rising of 1715, he could variously be described as clan chief, cattle drover and thief, bankrupt, folk hero, fugitive, prisoner, escapee and loyal subject – a varied career indeed!

Rob Roy died in 1734, a free man, and is buried with his wife and two of his sons at Balquhidder. His grave bears the words "A MacGregor Despite Them". Many features around Loch Lomond and The Trossachs bear his name, based both on reality and legend.

The Rob Roy Way, a seventy-nine mile (127km) long-distance path, begins at Drymen and continues to Pitlochry – Details from VisitScotland in Callander.

Nearby are ruins of a 1631 church and foundations of a 12th century one, thought to have been built over the grave of St. Angus. Excavations unearthed a skull complete with embedded musket ball – the remains thought to be of a Jacobite supporter on his way to join the 1745 uprising. Designed by David Bryce, the church was built in 1855 and paid for by David Carnegie who had become rich through brewing and sugar refining. His grave bears an unusual monument – a bottle of Carnegie "porter".

The graveyard's main attraction is the grave of Rob Roy MacGregor, his wife Helen and two of their sons. The location of other gravestones of interest are shown on a metal plaque. There are several of Clan McLaren, the MacGregors' chief rivals. McLarens ruled the glen for several hundred years before the MacGregors arrived.

The church has a beautiful wooden ceiling and ancient artefacts, including the

Rob Roy's Grave

stone which lay over the grave of St. Angus and a font found in the walls of the 17th century church. In a glass case are photocopies of an Irish Gaelic bible from 1688 and a New Testament published in 1690, translated by the Reverend Robert Kirke (see page 35).

The Boar's Hill: Behind the church is "The Boar's Hill". A stone monument marks where Clan MacLaren used to meet. Also here is "The Hill of Fire", either where people obtained a burning rush twice a year to relight their own fires or where the MacLarens rallied when the "fiery cross" was brandished.

Mhor Tea at The Old Library: Built by a local landowner to promote reading among his workers, this is now a tearoom serving traditional cream teas and delicious home-made scones. Open 10.00am – 5.00pm. Easter – End of Sep.

Balquhidder Glen & Loch Voil

Here tranquillity belies a violent past. Legend tells of one battle caused by a Buchanan slapping a MacLaren with a dead salmon! Many Buchanans were killed. Another incident saw an oath of secrecy being sworn over the severed head of a MacGregor victim. As well as fugitives and clan skirmishes, the glen was subject to the infamous "Clearances" when many families were forced to leave their homes.

The road runs through mixed woodland alongside Loch Voil in which are reflected the towering peaks on either side of the water. Half way along Loch Voil is "Bruce's Tree" – growing out of a rock by the shore. Picturesque waterfalls cascade down to join the loch, one at Monachyle having scoured large cauldron shaped hollows in the rock below the stone bridge.

Monachyle Mhor Hotel, once an 18th century farmhouse, is now a cosy but luxurious hotel, family owned and run.

The home farm supplies lamb, beef, pork, eggs and vegetables and the family also own a bakery and fishmongers. Venison is obtained from the nearby moorland above the glen.

Loch Voil is joined by a narrow stretch of water to tiny Loch Doine, into which flows the River Larig. Half a mile (0.8km) west is Ardcarnaig where there is a MacGregor burial ground. One of Rob Roy's earlier homes was at Monachyle Tuarach on the far shore where the two lochs meet.

Inverlochlarig is where the public road ends. The Inverlochlarig Estate is a 10,000 acre hill farm with a modern venison processing plant where wild venison can be purchased. The estate has provided a car park and shelter. Nearby are signed footpaths for climbing Beinn Tulaichean, Beinn a' Chroin, Stob Garbh, and several other peaks. Rob Roy lived out his later years at Inverlochlarig.

The MacGregor Murray Mausoleum: On the road linking Balquhidder to the A84, this ornate mausoleum was built around 1820 to house the remains of the Chief of the MacGregor Murrays.

The Kingshouse Hotel: Reputedly built in 1779 for the grand sum of £40.00, the hotel was originally a drovers' inn. After the building of the military road it was a stopping off place for soldiers. The Rob Roy Bar, complete with tartan seats, boasts a range of malt whiskies.

Sula Soft Furnishings, signposted from the A84, is the place to discover soft furnishings and gifts hand crafted from beautiful, traditional textiles such as Harris and Shetland Tweed. To see the lovingly restored signpost nearby is an added bonus.

Balquhidder Braes Holiday Park occupies the site of the old station, obsolete since the railway closed in 1965. Log cabins available all year, static caravans and tourers from Mar. to Nov.

The Golden Larches Restaurant is wheelchair friendly and serves food all day. Open Mar. – Oct.

Lochearnhead

The A84 and A85 meet here. There is a small village store at the head of the loch and a post office (the first one opened here in 1800) but visitors tend to congregate along the northern shore where the hotels and water sports are to be found.

Loch Earn – Northern Shore (described here from west to east)
The area has long been inhabited – the remains of a crannog from over two thousand years ago can be seen in the south west corner (a dwelling built on an

Loch Voil and Loch Doine

artificial island for security). The loch is 6.5 miles (10.5km) long, a mile (1.6km) wide and said to house to a mythical water horse. Loch Earn experiences a strange phenomenon: Although not connected to the sea it is "tidal" - the loch lies along the direction of the prevailing wind and the water is pushed to one end. Over a period of sixteen hours the water moves along the loch and back in a predictable and measurable tide, known as a "seiche". Loch Earn is one of the few Scottish lochs on which speedboats are permitted. There is a car park and several lay-bys on the north shore. Fishing permits are available from the village shop at St. Fillans.

Lochearnhead Hotel is a family run hotel with public bar and lovely views from The Lochview Restaurant. Open Feb – mid Dec.

Clachan Cottage Hotel is dog friendly, has its own slipway, jetty and moorings and can organise water sports and tuition directly from the hotel. Bar and restaurant open to non residents.

Lochearnhead Watersports Centre:

Lochearnhead Watersports Centre

Boat hire, water ski-ing, wake-boarding, knee-boarding, towable rides etc. Loch-side licensed restaurant.

St. Fillans

St. Fillan was a 6th century missionary. The village, largely built by the Drummond family in the 19th century, has attractive stone mansions and villas and a wide range of accommodation, places to eat and things to do and see. It developed as a resort with the arrival of the railway in 1903. Sir Walter Scott's "The Legend of Montrose" was set around St. Fillans, which had been known as The Port of Loch Earn or Meikleport until renamed in 1817 by Clementia Drummond.

The Four Seasons Hotel: Lime was extracted at St Fillans, one kiln still visible next to the hotel, originally the kiln manager's house. Award winning formal or informal dining. (Seasonal opening.)

Lime Kiln

The Scree Walk – Goats' Path: A board by the lime kiln shows the route for this circular walk with spectacular views over the loch and passing the entrance to the power station.

Achray House Hotel: Built in the 1800s and a guest house since the early 1900s, Achray House was once called "Victoria Cottage" after Queen Victoria commented on its attractiveness. The conservatory restaurant is renowned for contemporary Scottish food, locally produced. Dinner: Daily Feb – Nov. Lunch: weekends then daily in Summer.

Dundurn Parish Church, with a pretty gothic style porch, was designed by G.T.Ewing and built in 1878. It has a medieval stone font, lovely oak panelling and a pulpit carved with Celtic knotwork. The stained glass windows dedicated to St. John and St. Peter are particularly beautiful.

Loch Earn Castle (ruins) stands on a small island, once a stronghold of Clan MacNeish (a sept of Clan MacGregor). It was raided by "Smooth John MacNab" and his eleven brothers to regain some stolen Christmas provisions! They raided the island in a boat carried from Loch Tay but, too exhausted to carry the boat home again, abandoned it on the mountain. A walking stick made from the keel is said to be handed down through generations of MacNabs.

St. Fillans Village Store: If you cannot buy it here you probably don't really need it! The village store sells local produce and crafts,

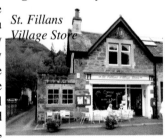
St. Fillans Village Store

yummy ice creams, fishing permits, kayak and boat hire. At the rear is the Braehead Galleries and Coffee Shop with home baking and speciality coffees.

The War Memorial enjoys views along the length of the loch.

The Old Church: At the eastern end of the village is this lovely old bluestone church, complete with bell tower. It was built in 1859 and is now self

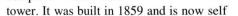
St. Fillans

catering accommodation.

St. Fillans Hydro-electric Power Station: Hidden from view above the village, this was tunnelled out of solid rock. Water from Loch Lednock, 3.5 miles (5.6km) north of St Fillans, is piped into the power station as part of the Breadalbane Power Scheme.

St. Fillans Dragon: By the side of the A85 beyond the east end of the village is St. Fillans Dragon, a rock decorated to "enhance" its natural shape. Watch also for St. Fillans Toad!

Loch Earn – Southern Shore (described here from east to west)

The road along the south side of the loch enjoys a more leisurely pace than the A85. From St. Fillans, the road crosses the River Earn which exits the loch to join the Tay Estuary 43 miles (70km) away. The south Loch Earn road is bordered on one side by steep woodland. There are several fishing jetties (permits necessary).

St Fillans Golf Club is a nine hole course with a licensed club house which welcomes visiting golfers. Club hire available.

Dundurn, a small hill near the golf course, was the site of a Pictish fort and also where St. Fillan lived. St Fillan's Chapel is in the Dundurn burial ground, where the Stewarts of Ardvorlich were interred.

The Loch Earn Leisure Park is a beautifully situated and extensive loch side park with holiday homes and facilities for touring caravans and motor-homes. Open Apr. – Oct.

James Stewart Memorial Stone: 3 miles (4.8km) along the road (GR 653235) is a memorial stone to James Stewart. On his death, Clan MacDonald avowed to desecrate the body on the way from Ardvorlich House to the funeral so his supporters hid the corpse in a shallow grave at this spot, where it remained for several years. Another roadside stone, near Ardvorlich, marks where remains of several MacDonalds were found – killed by the Stewarts during a MacDonald raid.

Memorial

Glen Vorlich joins the loch midway along its length and is a popular route for the ascent of mighty Ben Vorlich, some 985m (3231') high.

Edinample Castle (private) was mainly built in the 17th century by Black Duncan Campbell of Glenorchy. Legend tells of the ghost of an unfortunate architect, forced to walk for ever around a non-existent parapet which he omitted to provide and found himself flung off the roof by the disappointed Duncan!

Glen Ogle (map on next page)
From Lochearnhead the A85 winds its way up steep sided Glen Ogle, "The Valley of Dread", with views of a railway viaduct. The elegant, twelve arched bridge was completed in 1899 and is largely concrete with an outer shell of local

granite. The line's scheduled closure in 1965 was pre-empted by a rock-fall. It is now a scenic footpath and cycleway. At the top of the glen is a car park and picnic area with panoramic views towards Ben Lawers, 1214m (3983') high, and a

Glen Ogle Viaduct

memorial to two RAF airmen killed in 1994 when their Tornado jet crashed nearby.

Lix Toll: sits at the A85/A827 junction, one explanation for the name being that the camp of the Fifty-ninth Legion of Romans was here. (Roman numerals for 59 - LIX !) The "toll" part of the name is rather more obvious – the 19th century toll house stands at the junction. The A827 runs down Glen Dochart to Killin with its spectacular falls (see page 68).

Lix Toll Garage offers a breakdown service, Land Rover hire, fuel, drinks and snacks. Tel: 01567 820280.

9. LOCHEARNHEAD TO KILLIN & CRIANLARICH

From Lix Toll the A827 branches off to Killin at the western end of Loch Tay. The River Dochart makes a spectacular tumble through the centre of the village in a series of waterfalls – the route allegedly taken by poor Finn's headless corpse (see page 71).

Killin may owe its name to the fact that what was left of Finn (also called Fingal) was rescued by his followers and given a decent burial here. Other theories include the

The Falls of Dochart

Gaelic "Cill Fhionn" ("white church"). St. Fillan of Glen Dochart (not St. Fillan from Loch Earn) preached and healed here. He was attributed with special powers, one being an ability to generate light from his left arm in order to read the scriptures after dark! Associated with St. Fillan is a collection of healing stones, set on a bed of straw which is still renewed each Christmas Eve. The stones reputedly heal different ailments, depending on which body part the stone resembles.

Killin has a wide range of facilities, shops and accommodation. An excellent heritage trail, accompanied by a booklet "Killin: The Natural Meeting Place," makes an interesting way to explore.

The War Memorial features a beautifully detailed kilted soldier with his rifle "slung," not held at "reverse arms" as on some memorials.

Killin War Memorial

The Falls of Dochart: The best view is from the bridge.

The Falls of Dochart Inn dates from the 1800s and has open fires, a restaurant and

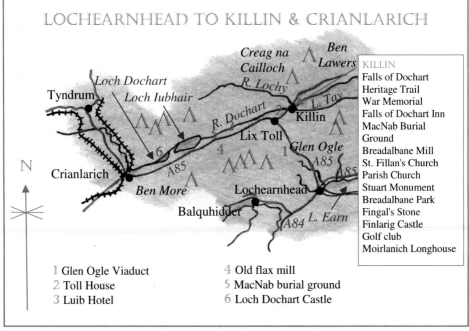

LOCHEARNHEAD TO KILLIN & CRIANLARICH

Creag na Cailloch

Ben Lawers

R. Lochy

Loch Dochart

Tyndrum

Loch Iubhair

R. Dochart

L. Tay

Killin

Lix Toll

A85

Glen Ogle

A85

Crianlarich

Ben More

Lochearnhead

Balquhidder

A84 L. Earn

N

KILLIN
Falls of Dochart
Heritage Trail
War Memorial
Falls of Dochart Inn
MacNab Burial Ground
Breadalbane Mill
St. Fillan's Church
Parish Church
Stuart Monument
Breadalbane Park
Fingal's Stone
Finlarig Castle
Golf club
Moirlanich Longhouse

1 Glen Ogle Viaduct
2 Toll House
3 Luib Hotel
4 Old flax mill
5 MacNab burial ground
6 Loch Dochart Castle

68

a candlelit bar serving real ales and featuring a collection of fascinating Jacobite swords. The inn has its own tearoom and gift shop. Canine friends welcome.

The MacNab Burial Ground is on the island Innis Bhuide in the middle of the river, accessed from the bridge. A notice tells

MacNab Burial Ground

where the key can be obtained. Seven MacNab Chiefs are buried here.

Breadalbane Mill, complete with water wheel, was built in 1840 on the site of an earlier mill built by St. Fillan.

The Old Smiddy Café Bistro operated as a smithy until the 1960s, having been built as such in 1886. Lovingly restored, it is now a cosy and welcoming coffee shop and bistro. (B & B also available in The Riverview Rooms.)

Bridge End Mill Gifts sell tartan, knitwear, souvenirs etc. (Seasonal.) Car park at rear.

The Main Street has an extensive range of shops: There is a fishmonger and fruiterer, bank, post office, pet food shop, galleries, antique and craft shops. There are also several cafés and restaurants and a supermarket.

PFK Garage: Vehicle repairs and breakdown service. Tel: 01567 829366

The Craigard Hotel, built in 1879, is open all year round. The Fishers Bar is a popular venue for live music. The restaurant serves reasonably priced Scottish fare.

First News sells magazines, newspapers, greetings cards etc.

Eureka: An excellent hardware shop which is like the proverbial Aladdin's Cave. Key cutting service.

Killin Outdoor Centre and Mountain Shop sells leading brands of outdoor clothing and has equipment for sale or hire. Local knowledge a speciality. Weather forecast available in shop or online. www.killinoutdoor.co.uk

St. Fillan's Episcopal Church is constructed of a wooden frame covered with corrugated iron. It was built in 1876 and is one of those referred as a "tin tabernacle".

The Parish Church: Built in 1744, this elegant church has an unusual hexagonal apse and beautiful stained glass windows. A smaller stained glass window depicts The Lilies of The Field (Matthew 6:28). The church has an ancient, seven sided stone font, rescued from the ruins of the old church and thought to be over a thousand years old. In a

Precious

glass case are replicas of two precious relics - the casing for the head of the crozier (staff) carried by St. Fillan and his bell. Open daily Easter – Oct.

The Stuart Monument, adjacent to the church, is dedicated to the Reverend James Stuart, who worked on the translation of The New Testament into Gaelic in 1767.

The Killin Hotel overlooks the river on the site of a former 17th century coaching inn. Serving food all day, there is a choice of formal dining or "bistro" type meals.

Breadalbane Park has a children's play

Stuart Monument & Killin Hotel

area and a bowling green, tennis courts and putting green open daily to visitors during Jul. and Aug.

Time Capsule: On the edge of Breadalbane Park is a time capsule containing community records, erected on the 1st of January 2001.

Fingal's Stone is said to have marked the spot where the giant was buried, after his demise (see page 71) and subsequent waterborne journey to Killin. The stone is behind the primary school, at the edge of Breadalbane Park, moved here from higher up the hill in the late 19th century.

The Coach House Hotel, originally stables, serves real ales and home cooked food all day. Live music nights weekly from Apr. – Oct.

Maragowan Caravan Club Site, on the banks of the River Lochy, is within easy walking distance of the village centre. The site enjoys access to the river for fishing – no permit needed. Calor gas stockist. Non members welcome. Open Mar. – Oct.

Loch Tay: Until 1939 a scheduled steamer service ran from a pier on Loch Tay. Current access to the loch is via the old railway or down Pier Road.

Finlarig Castle: This was another of Black Sir Duncan Campbell's castles (see page 71), built in the early 1620s. The ruins are along the track to the loch . Nearby are the graves of Sir Gavin and Lady Campbell. The buildings are in a dangerous state.

The Bridge of Lochay Hotel is an original 1765 coaching inn with wonderful oak beams and panelling. (Note the service call lights in the reception area.) The hotel serves fine

Bridge Of Lochay Hotel

Scottish produce cooked with flair and imagination, including home smoking.

Killin Golf Club is a picturesque, if somewhat hilly, nine hole course which welcomes visitors. Bar and restaurant open to non golfers. Open all year.

Moirlanich Longhouse is a preserved Scottish cruck frame longhouse, where family and cattle lived under the same roof. It was occupied by the

Moirlanich Longhouse

same family from the 19th century until 1968, now owned by The National Trust for Scotland. In the hut next door is an exhibition of clothes found in the longhouse. Open Wed. and Sun. 2.00pm. – 5.00pm May - Sept.

Glen Dochart

West of Lix Toll the A85 runs the length of Glen Dochart with Ben More (height 1174m/3852') to the south west.

The Old Flax Mill: Flax (linseed) has pretty blue flowers and tough fibrous stems, the fibres from which are spun to make linen. The mill was sited here for the supply of water from the River Dochart and marshy land where flax would flourish. On the opposite side of the road were cottages to house the workers. The converted mill houses a coffee stop, restaurant and takeaway, with a popular carvery at weekends. Open from 11.00am. Feb – Dec. (closed Tue. & Wed.)

The Luib Hotel is an original drovers' inn from the mid 1600s. Full of character with roaring log fires, it offers comfortable accommodation, food served all day and a large choice of malt whiskies.

The Suie Lodge Hotel was originally a shooting lodge. The word "suie" means "seat" or "headquarters" and it was from here that St. Fillan is thought to have based his evangelical travels. Open all year, dog friendly, lunches and evening meals available to non residents. Deep freeze service available to anglers staying here.

MacNab Burial Ground: Opposite the Suie Lodge Hotel, on a small rise, is an enclosed burial ground of the MacNabs of Innishewan - a hamlet just across the river. A slab bearing a carved cross sign is thought to date from the 6th or 7th century.

Glendochart Caravan Park is family run and has static caravans for hire as well as welcoming tents and touring caravans. Open Mar. – Nov.

Loch Iubhair: Different tales link the loch with either a leper or someone sly. It is a small loch, not quite 1.5 miles (2.4km) long and joined to Loch Dochart by a short stretch of river.

Ben More: Just east of Ben More Farm is the start of the path up this Munro climbing steeply up Ben More Glen to the summit at 1174m (3851').

Portnellan Lodges: Based around a Victorian hunting lodge, the attractive grounds now have log cabin accommodation with a large range of outdoor activities available on and off the site. Fishing permits available here.

Loch Dochart, east of Crianlarich, is tiny and atmospheric. Loch Dochart Castle, on a small island, was built about four hundred years ago by Black Sir Duncan Campbell (who is said to have built castles as a hobby!) An earlier inhabitant is said to have been Giant Taileachd, whose arch enemy was Giant Finn. Both loved the same woman. To settle the matter they held a competition jumping backwards from the island to the shore (as one does!) Finn landed in the water and had his head cut off by Taileachd. The headless body then floated down Glen Dochart to Killin.

Crianlarich - see page 19

Public Toilets
St Fillans – opposite lay by west of the village
Killin – signposted from the bridge
Wi-Fi
Ben More Lodge hotel near Crianlarich

INDEX OF PLACE NAMES

NOTES